1000
Ideas for
CREATIVE
REUSE

QUARRY

Remake, Restyle, Recycle, Renew

1000 Ideas for
Ideas for
CREATIVE
REUSE

GARTH JOHNSON

BEVERLY MASSACHUSETTS

QUARRY BOOKS

2008

First published in the United States of America by
Quarry Books, a member of
Quayside Publishing Group
100 Cummings Center
Suite 406-L
Beverly, Massachusetts 01915-6101
Telephone: (978) 282-9590
Fax: (978) 283-2742
www.quarrybooks.com
Visit www.Craftside.Typepad.com for a behind-the-scenes peek at our crafty world!

Library of Congress Cataloging-in-Publication Data
Johnson, Garth.
  1000 ideas for creative reuse : remake, restyle, recycle, renew / Garth Johnson.
     p. cm.
  ISBN-13: 978-1-59253-540-8
  ISBN-10: 1-59253-540-2
  1. Handicraft. 2. Salvage (Waste, etc.) I. Title.
  TT157.J594 2009
  745.5—dc22

                                              2009016050

ISBN-13: 978-1-59253-540-8
ISBN-10: 1-59253-540-2

10 9 8 7 6 5 4 3 2 1

Design: Sandra Salamony
Cover and title page art: Bryant Holsenbeck

Printed in China

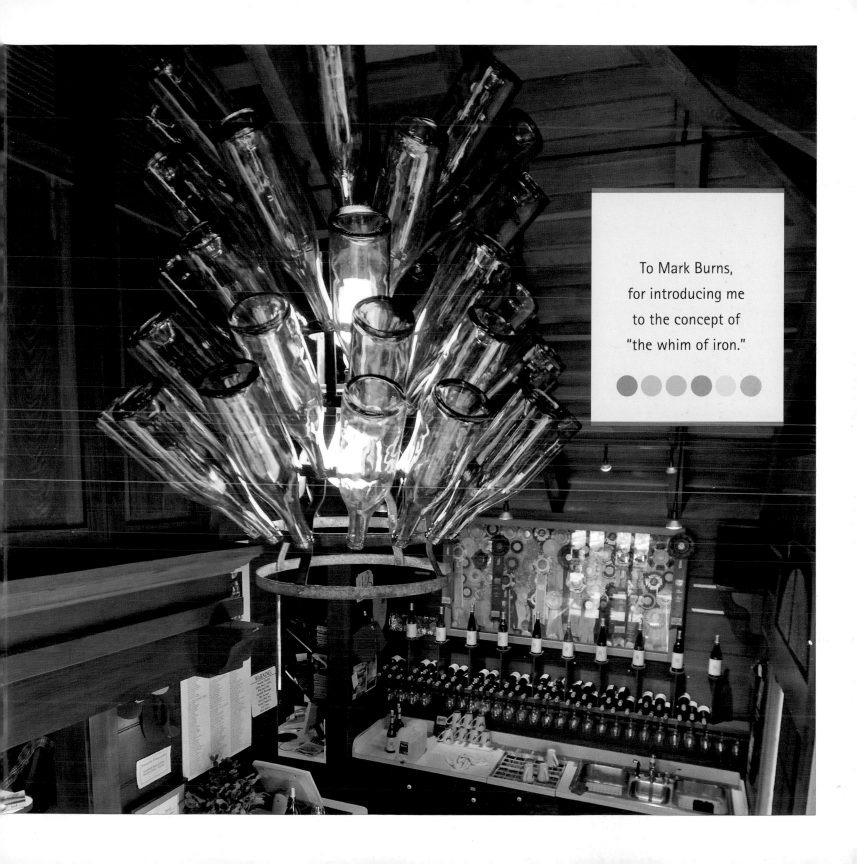

To Mark Burns,
for introducing me
to the concept of
"the whim of iron."

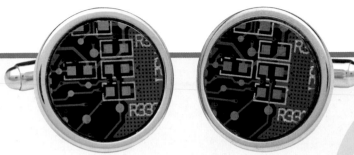

contents

introduction

DURING THE LAST WEEKS OF GATHERING IMAGES FOR THIS BOOK, I took a short trip with my wife to visit some wineries near Mendocino, California. When we walked into the Navarro Winery in Philo, I saw an object that summed up everything that I loved about creative reuse. The gallery owners had taken an antique bottle drying rack, covered it with wine bottles, and converted it into a light fixture. It took me a few moments to realize why the wine rack looked so familiar.

The light fixture, stripped of its bottles and lights, was almost identical to Marcel Duchamp's 1914 "readymade" entitled *Bottle Dryer* or *Hedgehog*, which can be seen at the Philadelphia Museum of Art. Duchamp's readymade sculptures were revolutionary because they challenged the orthodoxy of the *objet d'art*. By taking ordinary objects and presenting them as "art," Duchamp ushered in the era of conceptual art. The winery owner at Navarro simply added another twist by lighting their tasting room with an icon of twentieth-century art.

Marcel Duchamp didn't invent creative reuse. In fact, medieval scribes regularly scraped off and reused parchments for their illuminated manuscripts. The ancient Greeks melted down older bronze statues to make newer, more naturalistic ones. Medieval Baghdad supposedly owed its splendor to architectural and decorative elements taken from ancient Babylonian sites. The Romans were the undisputed champions of reuse. They re-carved marble statues of disgraced emperors into statues of emperors with better reputations. The Romans even pillaged decorative elements from monuments and buildings to make new monuments such as the Arch of Constantine, conveniently "re-branding" the characters and symbols to make them fit into their new environs.

Christian cultures embraced creative reuse with equal vigor, superimposing their beliefs and architecture on Roman foundations, both figurative and literal. Early Christians adapted Roman temples into places of worship, decorating them with motifs like Dionysian grapes repurposed to symbolize the blood of Christ. Later churches continued this tradition of reuse. St. Mark's Basilica in Venice is a striking example, covered not only in columns and decorations from the Romans and Greeks, but also from their trading partners in Asia and the Middle East.

Throughout history, the reuse of materials meant different things to different cultures. Sometimes, the reuse of materials showed the dominance of one culture over another. The spoils of war were integrated into buildings as mementos of victory. Other times, reused materials were used to establish a link with classical antiquity. The classical columns in St. Peter's Basilica in Rome are meant to hearken back to the grandeur of ancient Rome.

Finally, and perhaps most importantly, the reuse of materials is about thrift. Ancient cultures from Egypt to India regularly "recycled" their buildings, sculptures, and objects out of convenience and necessity. Whenever resources become scarce, creative reuse becomes second nature.

A more recent example of creative reuse comes from the Werkbund, a German association of designers founded in 1907. The Werkbund was designed to educate the German people about the beauty of well-designed objects. The group offered their minimal designs as an alternative to the mass-marketed objects of popular taste. In the lean years after World War II, Werkbund members embraced the creative reuse of war material. The Werkbund's archive, the Museum der Dinge (Museum of Things) in Berlin contains beautiful examples of gas masks refashioned into candlestick holders and helmets that have been enameled and turned into cooking pots. The objects are hardly the minimal designs of the original Werkbund, but they are elegant in their simple utility.

1000 Ideas for Creative Reuse has been a joy to curate. As unlikely as it seems, out of the many thousands of brilliant examples submitted, it was hard to limit myself to 1,000. The book contains examples of all three types of reuse I cited earlier: dominance, heritage, and thrift.

Like Duchamp's readymades, artists like Margaux Lange (Images 343-348) and Stuart Karsten (Image 691) take iconic objects like Barbie dolls and dollar bills and subjugate them to their own vision, fashioning something surprising and new out of objects that are so common as to be invisible. The viewer (or user) is delighted by the designer's clever use of pedestrian materials.

Like the architects of St. Peters, other artists reuse objects to evoke the past. The burgeoning "steampunk" movement is well-represented in this book. The steampunk movement is based around creating familiar objects that are immaculately crafted using Victorian-era technology. Gears and clockwork hearken back to an era that predates disposable silicone chips. Artist Richard Nagy (Image 536) even houses modern, faceless computers in handsome brass, copper, and wood enclosures that would melt the heart of even the most recalcitrant technophobe.

Finally, most of the projects in *1000 Ideas for Creative Reuse* are thrifty…or downright ecological. One of the joys of reading this book is guessing the materials used in each project (they are listed in the image directory, page 305). This book contains photographs of literally *tons* of objects that have escaped the cruel fate of the landfill. It is the desire to transform the everyday cast-off into something extraordinary that is the thread holding this book together.

I consider everything in this book to be art, however, as a concession to organization, I have broken down the chapters into: paper goods and assemblage; couture and soft goods; jewelry and adornment; geek craft and man craft; housewares and furnishings; and art, interiors, and installations. Because of the overlap between categories, deciding which category to place objects in has been as nerve-wracking as planning the seating chart for a society wedding dinner. As I've been biting my fingernails down to the quick over these decisions, somewhere, I suspect, Marcel Duchamp is laughing his ass off.

Enjoy,
Garth Johnson

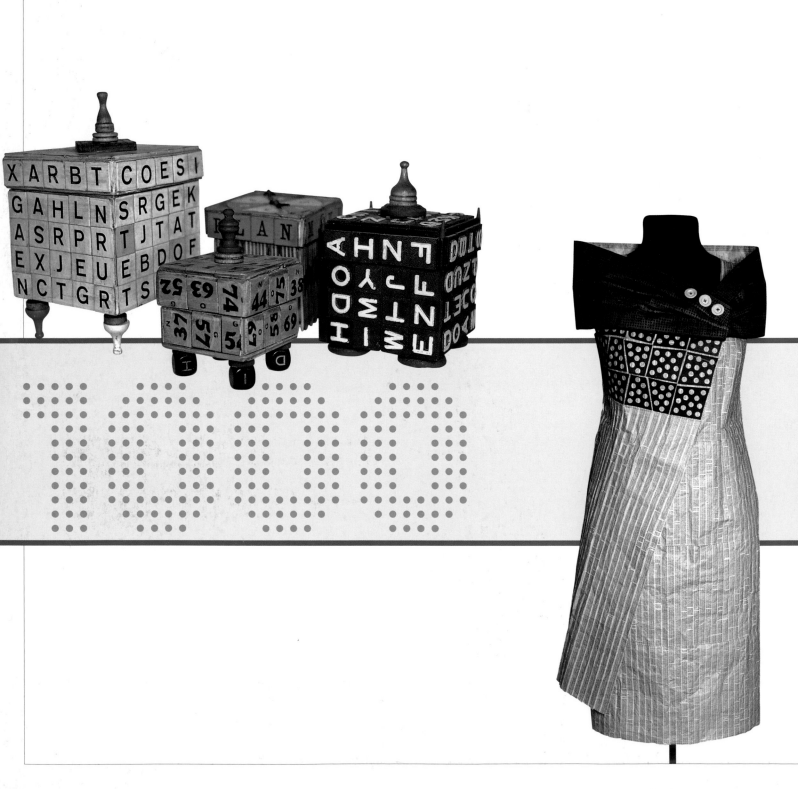

paper, collage +assemblage

0001–0101

PHOTO BY JOHN POLAK PHOTOGRAPHY

0001   JOYCE ROSENFELD, USA

0002 SUSAN DWYER, UP IN THE AIR SOMEWHERE, USA

0003 EVA BUCHALA, LADY ARTISAN, USA

0004 SUSAN DWYER, UP IN THE AIR SOMEWHERE, USA

0005 SUSAN DWYER, UP IN THE AIR SOMEWHERE, USA

0006 VALERIE ARNTZEN, CANADA

0007 MICHELLE PUGH, SMASHGIRL MOSIACS, USA

PHOTO BY BRUCE MACGREGOR

0008 CONNIE JEUNG-MILLS, USA

0009 ELAINE G. CHU, USA

0011   MEGAN K. HOFFMAN, FRANK & GERTRUDE, THE NETHERLANDS

0012 DIANE GILLELAND, CRAFTYPOD, USA

0013 ELKE URSIN, SWEET TWEE LAB, USA

0014 RUTH FIEGE, USA

0015 MEGAN K. HOFFMAN, FRANK & GERTRUDE, THE NETHERLANDS

0016 JULIE McNIEL, USA

0017 MEGAN K. HOFFMAN, FRANK & GERTRUDE, THE NETHERLANDS

0018 KRISTA STUMPH, CANADA

0019 GIRL INDUSTRIES, UK

0020 AMY RUBIN FLETT, CANADA

0021 CAMILLE ASSERAF, USA

0022 KRISTA STUMPH, CANADA

0023 ALISON WILDER, USA

0025 CARROLL M. WOODS, USA

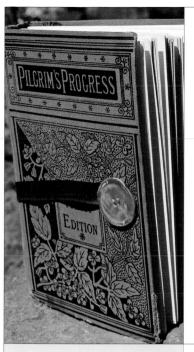

0026 MANDY FARIELLO, USA

0027 YOUR SECRET ADMIRAL, USA

0028 KRISTA STUMPH, CANADA

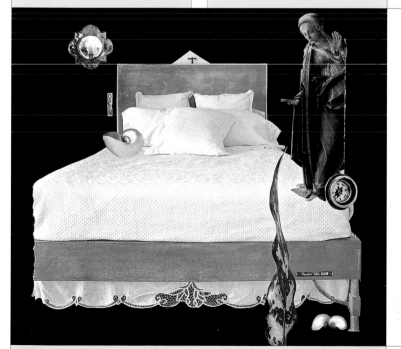

PHOTO BY JOHN POLAK PHOTOGRAPHY

0029 JOYCE ROSENFELD, USA

0030 BECKY HAWLEY, USA

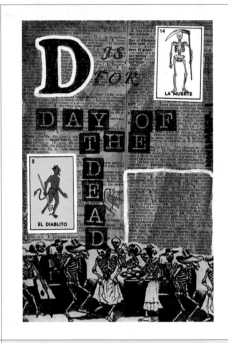

0031 KRISTA STUMPH, CANADA

0032 BECKY HAWLEY, USA

0033 CARROLL M. WOODS, USA

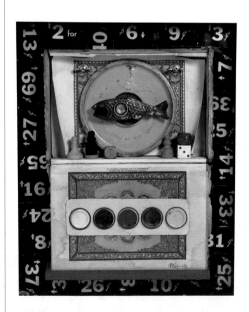

0034 KRISTA STUMPH, CANADA

0035 RUTH FIEGE, USA

0036 CARROLL M. WOODS, USA

0037 VALERIE THAI, CABIN + CUB DESIGN, CANADA

0038   DIANE GILLELAND, CRAFTYPOD, USA

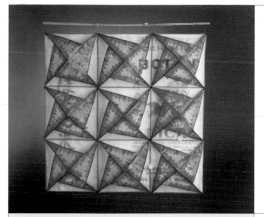 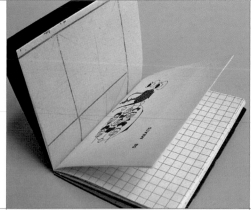 

| 0039 | CORINNE OKADA TAKARA, USA | 0040 | YOUR SECRET ADMIRAL, USA | 0041 | HEATHER LEA BIRDSALL, VERDOLOGY, USA |

 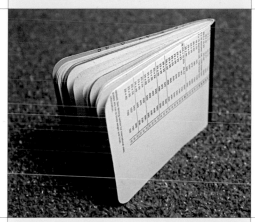 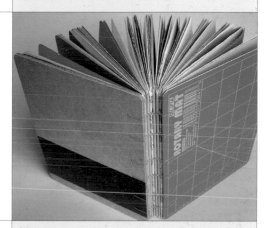

| 0042 | CHRISTY PETTERSON, A BARDIS, USA | 0043 | HEATHER LEA BIRDSALL, VERDOLOGY, USA | 0044 | YOUR SECRET ADMIRAL, USA |

  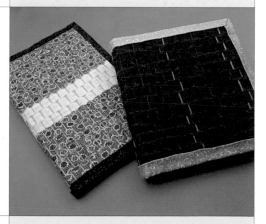

| 0045 | HEATHER LEA BIRDSALL, VERDOLOGY, USA | 0046 | YOUR SECRET ADMIRAL, USA | 0047 | DIANE GILLELAND, CRAFTYPOD, USA |

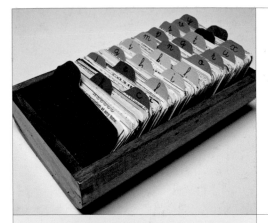

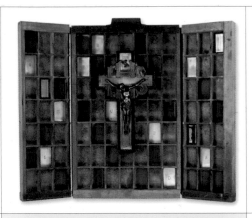

0048 RENEE DE SIBOUR, MY UGLY KITTY, USA

0049 VALERIE ARNTZEN, CANADA

0050 RUTH FIEGE, USA

0051 YOUR SECRET ADMIRAL, USA

0052 RUTH FIEGE, USA

0053 LAUREL NATHANSON, USA

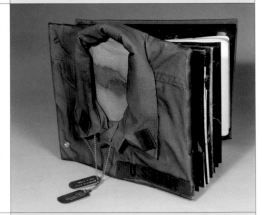

0054 MEGAN K. HOFFMAN, FRANK & GERTRUDE, THE NETHERLANDS

0055 MOLLY B. RIGHT, USA

0056 WENDY JORDAN, USA

0057 MOLLY B. RIGHT, USA

0058 DIANE GILLELAND, CRAFTYPOD, USA

0059 LISA KIRKPATRICK, AUSTRALIA

0060 LISA KIRKPATRICK, AUSTRALIA

0061 LISA KIRKPATRICK, AUSTRALIA

0062 RUTH FIEGE, USA

0063 VALERIE THAI, CABIN + CUB DESIGN, CANADA

0064 VALERIE THAI, CABIN + CUB DESIGN, CANADA

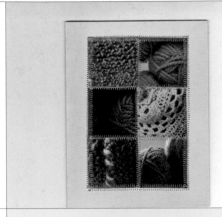

0065 HEATHER PRICE,
WINEMAKERSSISTER, USA

0066 HEATHER PRICE,
WINEMAKERSSISTER, USA

0067 HEATHER LEA BIRDSALL,
VERDOLOGY, USA

"Drop it," Lach told him quietly.
Then Lach put his arm around Richard and the pair
left a Canadien dressing room together for the last time.
"I would have given five years of my life to have scored
just one more goal," said Lach.

0068 KRISTY ATHENS, USA

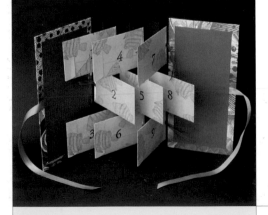

0069 ELAINE G. CHU, USA

0070 ATYPYK, FRANCE

0071 MEGAN KLEPP, TA-DAH, USA

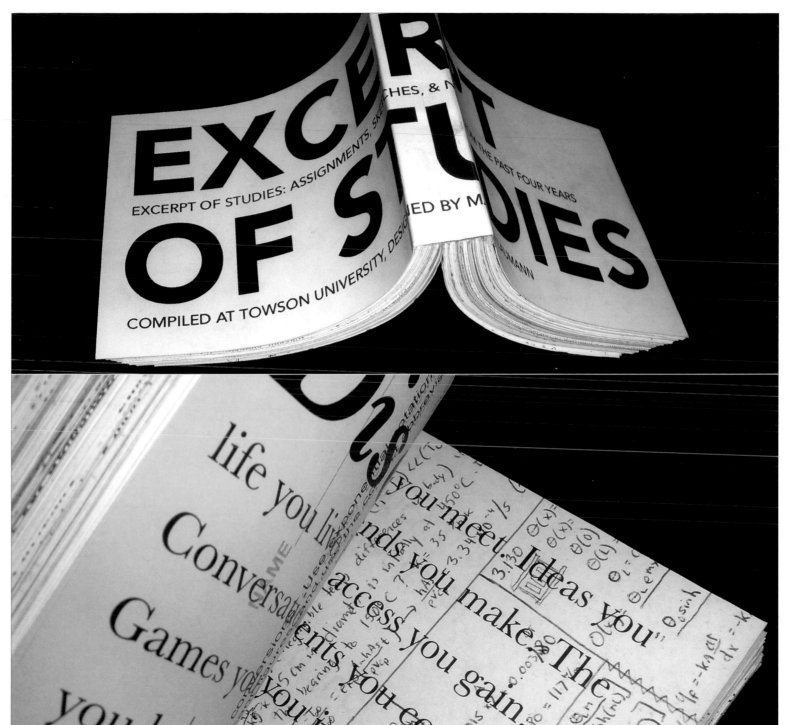

0073 EVA BUCHALA, LADY ARTISAN, USA

0074 WENDY JORDAN, USA

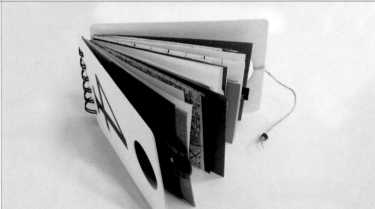

0075 CARROLL M. WOODS, USA

0076 BECKY HAWLEY, USA

0077 JULIE McNIEL, USA

0078 KRISTA STUMPH, CANADA

0080 JANET LEE, JANET PLANET DESIGNS, CANADA

0081 JANET LEE, JANET PLANET DESIGNS, CANADA

0082 JANET LEE, JANET PLANET DESIGNS, CANADA

0083 KEN FLETT, CANADA

0084 CORINNE OKADA TAKARA, USA

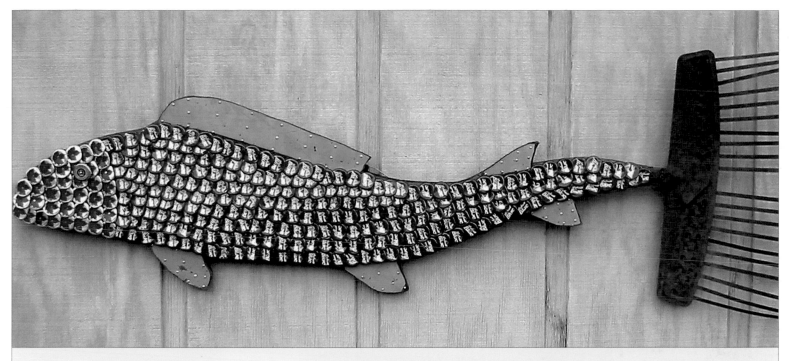

0085 JOHN T. UNGER, USA

0086 JYLIAN GUSTLIN, USA

0087 JOHN T. UNGER, USA

0088 JYLIAN GUSTLIN, USA

0089 KRISTY ATHENS, USA

0090 QUEEN COQUETTE,
THE TABBY CAT, USA

0091 JOANNE ZDROJEWSKI, USA

0092 CAMILLE ASSERAF, USA

0093 JYLIAN GUSTLIN, USA

0094 JYLIAN GUSTLIN, USA

0095   LAUREL NATHANSON, USA

0096   JEANNE TREMEL, USA

0097   JULIE McNIEL, USA

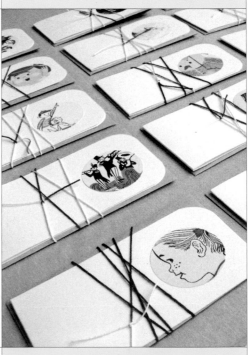

0098   CARROLL M. WOODS, USA

0099   HUW BRISCOE, UNFOLD STUDIO, UK

0100   VALERIE THAI, CABIN + CUB DESIGN, CANADA

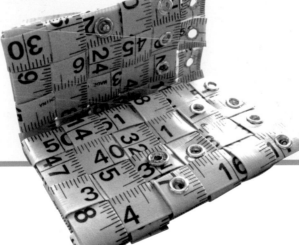

couture+
soft goods

0102–0314

0102   KATHRYN WILSON, JUNKHOUSE DOLLYARD DESIGNS, JAPAN

0103 KATHRYN WILSON, JUNKHOUSE DOLLYARD DESIGNS, JAPAN

0104 KATHRYN WILSON, JUNKHOUSE DOLLYARD DESIGNS, JAPAN

PHOTO BY TAURA HORN

0105 JESSICA PLYMATE, AORTA APPAREL, USA

0106 KATHRYN WILSON, JUNKHOUSE DOLLYARD DESIGNS, JAPAN

0107 NIFTY THRIFTY, UK

0108 ALICIA L. WOODS, USA

0109 SANDY DROBNY, USA

0110 NOTTYPOOCH DESIGN, MALAYSIA

0111 CRISTINA POULOPOULOU, GREECE

0112 KATE BINGAMAN-BURT, USA

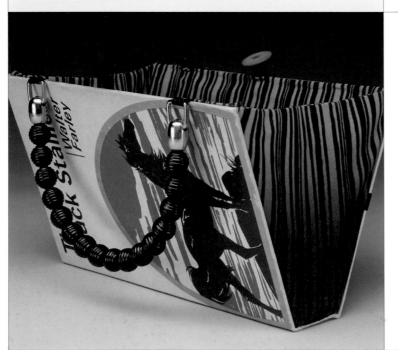

0113 CAITLIN PHILLIPS, REBOUND DESIGN, USA

0114 RENE KREIS, USA

0115 SANDY DROBNY, USA

0116 ANNA RADDATZ, USA

0117 HELEN CARTER, SECRET LENTIL, USA

0118 SHANNON MULKEY, PATINA, USA

0119 SHANNON MULKEY, PATINA, USA

0120 EMU IZAKI, NEW ZEALAND

0121 MERILL COMEAU, USA

0122 MERILL COMEAU, USA

0123 MERILL COMEAU, USA

0124 MERILL COMEAU, USA

0125 WINDY WISE STINER, THE PETTICOAT PIRATE, USA

0126 ODELIA MAKES DOLLS, ISRAEL

0127 COLLEEN MARIA CASEY, USA

0128 COLLEEN MARIA CASEY, USA

0129 COLLEEN MARIA CASEY, USA

0130 LEE MEREDITH, LEETHAL, USA

0131   CLAIRE JOYCE, USA

0132 ANNIKA GINSBERG, MAHKA CRAFT, USA

0133 LAURA HAWKER PLOUZEK, XOELLE, USA

0134 LEE MEREDITH, LEETHAL, USA

0135 KATHERINE RASMUSSEN, REITER8, USA

0136 PRIYA MANI, DENMARK

0137 STEPHANIE SYJUCO, ANTI-FACTORY, USA

0138 KATHERINE RASMUSSEN, REITER8, USA

0139 LAURA HAWKER PLOUZEK, XOELLE, USA

0140 NANCY GAMON, USA

0141　JESSICA PLYMATE, AORTA APPAREL, USA

PHOTO BY TAURA HORN

0142　JESSICA PLYMATE, AORTA APPAREL, USA

PHOTO BY TAURA HORN

0143　JESSICA PLYMATE, AORTA APPAREL, USA

PHOTO BY TAURA HORN

0144　JESSICA PLYMATE, AORTA APPAREL, USA

PHOTO BY TAURA HORN

PHOTO BY TAURA HORN

0146   ELIZABETH LUNDBERG MORISETTE, USA

0148 SHANNON MULKEY, PATINA, USA

0149 SANDY DROBNY, USA

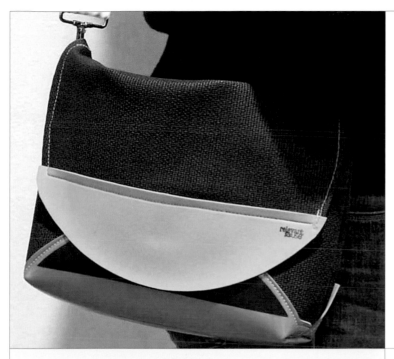

0150 HEATHER YOUGHDAHL MULLINS, USA

0151 LISA ORGLER DESIGN, USA

PHOTO BY NICOLA CHAPPELL

0152 POUCH, UK

0153 ANGSTY TEENAGE ECO WARRIORS, USA

0154 MANDY CURL,
MANDINKA DESIGNS, USA

0155 MANDY CURL,
MANDINKA DESIGNS, USA

0156 MANDY CURL,
MANDINKA DESIGNS, USA

0157 MANDY CURL,
MANDINKA DESIGNS, USA

0158 MANDY CURL,
MANDINKA DESIGNS, USA

0159 MANDY CURL,
MANDINKA DESIGNS, USA

0161 RAUL SIRO FERREIRA, USA

PHOTO BY JENN GREEN

COUTURE + SOFT GOODS

61

0163 RAUL SIRO FERREIRA, USA

0164 SHANNON MULKEY, PATINA, USA

0165 RAUL SIRO FERREIRA, USA

0166 RAUL SIRO FERREIRA, USA

0167   KATHERINE RASMUSSEN, REITER8, USA

0168   KATHRYN WILSON, JUNKHOUSE DOLLYARD DESIGNS, JAPAN

0170 HOLLAND SEYDEL, HAUTE NATURE, USA

0171 JULIE FLOERSCH, USA

0169 MICHELLE HANSEN, UNDONE CLOTHING, USA

0172 1MIND1, HUNGARY

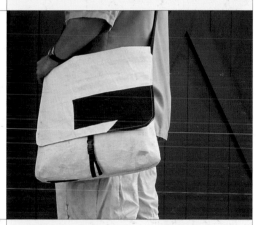

0173 KATHERINE RASMUSSEN, REITER8, USA

0174 FAITH AND JUSTINA BLAKENEY, COMPAI DESIGN STUDIO INC., USA

0175 JUDY TITCHE, REZOOM, USA

0176 JUDY TITCHE, REZOOM, USA

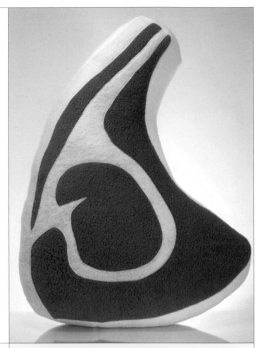

0177 LAUREN VENELL,
SWEET MEATS, USA

0178 LAUREN VENELL,
SWEET MEATS, USA

0179 LAUREN VENELL,
SWEET MEATS, USA

0180 OUISSI, BRITISH CREAM TEA, UK

0181 OUISSI, BRITISH CREAM TEA, UK

0182 LEE MEREDITH, LEETHAL, USA

0183 MEANBEAN, USA

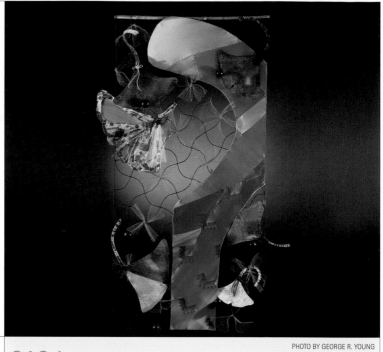

0184 CORINNE OKADA TAKARA, USA

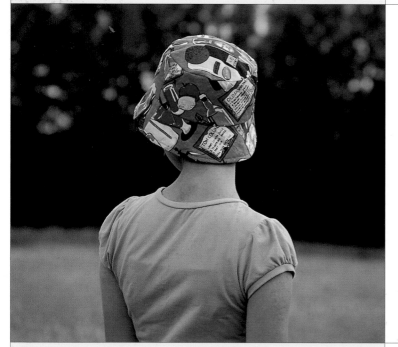

0185 EMU IZAKI, NEW ZEALAND

0186 CARROLL M. WOODS, USA

1000 IDEAS FOR CREATIVE REUSE

0187 IRINA NUNEZ, USA

0188 IRINA NUNEZ, USA

0189 DAVID CRAFT, GOGREENCRAFT, USA

0190 IRINA NUNEZ, USA

0191   MAE HENRY, USA

PHOTO BY NICOLE JEAN HILL

0192 ODELIA MAKES DOLLS, ISRAEL

0193 VELMA ROOT,
COLORBOMB CREATIONS, USA

0194 CLAIRE JOYCE, USA

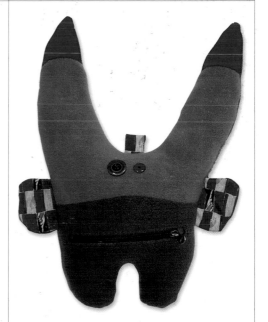

0195 YESDESIGNGROUP, USA

0196 SANDY DROBNY, USA

COUTURE + SOFT GOODS

71

0197 AMY QUARRY, CANADA

0198 AMY QUARRY, CANADA

0199 AMY QUARRY, CANADA

0200 AMY QUARRY, CANADA

0201 LARA NEWSOM, HANDMADE PRETTIES, USA

0202 IRINA NUNEZ, USA

0203   FAITH AND JUSTINA BLAKENEY, COMPAI DESIGN STUDIO INC., USA

0204 CHRISTINA L. WRIGHT, USA

0205 SARAH PERRY, USA

COUTURE + SOFT GOODS

0206 TAKE OFF YOUR CLOTHES, USA

0207 STEPHANIE SYJUCO, ANTI-FACTORY, USA

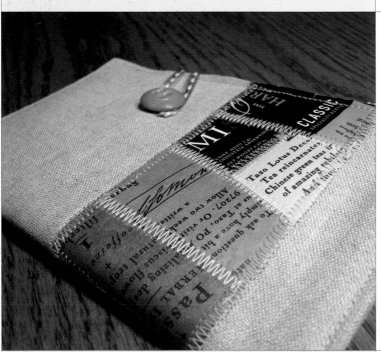

0208 HEATHER PRICE, WINEMAKERSSISTER, USA

0209 CLAIRE JOYCE, USA

0210   KATHRYN WILSON, JUNKHOUSE DOLLYARD DESIGNS, JAPAN

0211   SHANNON MULKEY, PATINA, USA

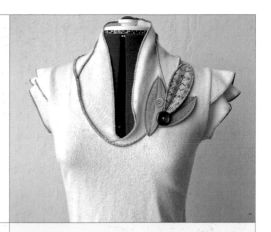

0212 POUCH, UK

0213 HELEN CARTER,
SECRET LENTIL, USA

0214 STEPHANIE SYJUCO,
ANTI-FACTORY, USA

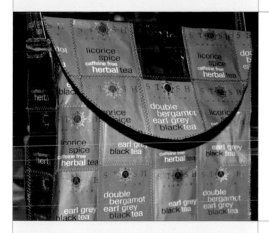

0215 MANDY FARIELLO, USA

0216 KATY CAMPBELL,
SHUTTERKATE, USA

0217 ANDREA SCHNEEBERG, USA

0218 KAT BOWES,
THISTLEDOWN & FINCH, USA

0219 SWEATER HOSPITAL
BY FIBREVOLUTION, USA

0220 CRISTINA POULOPOULOU,
GREECE

COUTURE + SOFT GOODS

0221   NIFTY THRIFTY, UK

0222   MEANBEAN, USA

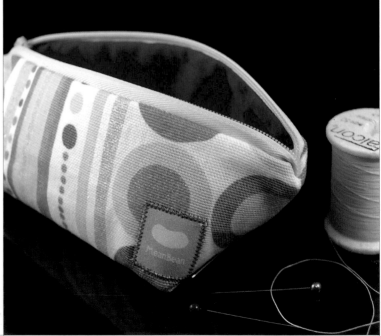

0223   JULEE DUNEKACKE JAEGER, USA

0224   MEANBEAN, USA

0226   CAITLIN PHILLIPS, REBOUND DESIGN, USA

0227 CAITLIN PHILLIPS, REBOUND DESIGN, USA

0228 CAITLIN PHILLIPS, REBOUND DESIGN, USA

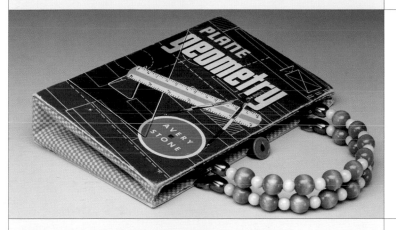

0229 CAITLIN PHILLIPS, REBOUND DESIGN, USA

0230 CAITLIN PHILLIPS, REBOUND DESIGN, USA

0231 RACHEL CHEZLIN BENEFIEL, USA

0232 BETTY MAPLE, USA

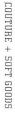

0233 1MIND1, HUNGARY

0234 SWEATER HOSPITAL, FIBREVOLUTION, USA

0235 GGRIPPO, TRASH-À-PORTER, USA

0236 JOSIE MARSH, WOOLY BABY, USA

0237 SUSAN CARLSON SKALAK, USA

0238 SARAH-MARIA VISCHER, USA

0239 HELEN CARTER, SECRET LENTIL, USA

0240 SWEATER HOSPITAL, FIBREVOLUTION, USA

0241　ANNA RADDATZ, USA

0242　JULEE DUNEKACKE JAEGER, USA

0243　DAVID CRAFT,
GOGREENCRAFT, USA

0244　EMU IZAKI, NEW ZEALAND

0245　ANDREA SCHNEEBERG, USA

0247 VELMA ROOT, COLORBOMB
CREATIONS, USA

0246 SHANNON MULKEY, PATINA, USA

0248 VELMA ROOT, COLORBOMB
CREATIONS, USA

0249 LEE MEREDITH, LEETHAL, USA

0250 LEE MEREDITH, LEETHAL, USA

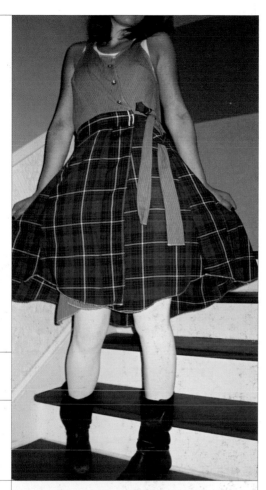

0251 HEIDI BROWN, HEIDALA'S, USA

0252 MARY ELLEN COUMERILH, USA

0253 DAVID CRAFT, GOGREENCRAFT, USA

0254 NOTTYPOOCH DESIGN, MALAYSIA

0255 NOTTYPOOCH DESIGN, MALAYSIA

0256 GGRIPPO, TRASH-A-PORTER, USA

0257 2REVERT, CANADA

0258 NOTTYPOOCH DESIGN, MALAYSIA

0259 FAITH AND JUSTINA BLAKENEY, COMPAI DESIGN STUDIO INC., USA

0260 LARA NEWSOM, HANDMADE PRETTIES, USA

0261 VELMA ROOT, COLORBOMB CREATIONS, USA

0262 ANGSTY TEENAGE ECO WARRIORS, USA

0263 ANGSTY TEENAGE ECO WARRIORS, USA

0264 BRIANNA MELI, MELT BRIANNA, USA

0265 STEPHANIE SYJUCO, ANTI-FACTORY, USA

0266 JUDY TITCHE, REZOOM, USA

0267 JUDY TITCHE, REZOOM, USA

0268 NANCY GAMON, USA

0269 NANCY GAMON, USA

0270 JOSIE MARSH, WOOLY BABY, USA

0271 NANCY GAMON, USA

0272 ROBYN L. COBURN,
IGGY JINGLES CRAFTS, USA

0273 CHICA AND JO, USA

0274 PRIYA MANI, DENMARK

0275 STEPHANIE SYJUCO,
ANTI-FACTORY, USA

0276 WINDY WISE STINER,
THE PETTICOAT PIRATE, USA

0277 EMU IZAKI, NEW ZEALAND

0278 MELANIE YOUNG,
PIECES OF YOU, AUSTRALIA

0279 MELANIE YOUNG,
PIECES OF YOU, AUSTRALIA

0280 MELANIE YOUNG,
PIECES OF YOU, AUSTRALIA

0281 MELANIE YOUNG,
PIECES OF YOU, AUSTRALIA

0282 IRINA NUNEZ, USA

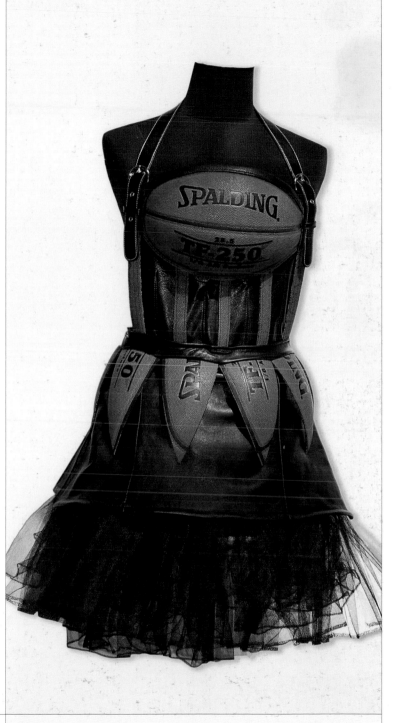

0283 SANDY DROBNY, USA

0284 SANDY DROBNY, USA

0285 MICHELLE HANSEN, UNDONE CLOTHING, USA

0286 LISA WINTER, USA

PHOTO BY NICOLA CHAPPELL

0287 BRIANNA MELI, MELT BRIANNA, USA

0288 POUCH, UK

0289 MEANBEAN, USA

PHOTO BY MICHAEL BURTON

0290 ANNE BURTON, USA

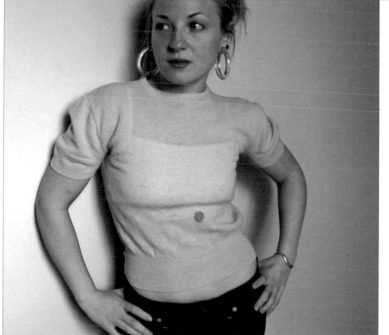

PHOTO BY GWEN REICHERT

0291 SWEATER HOSPITAL BY FIBREVOLUTION, USA

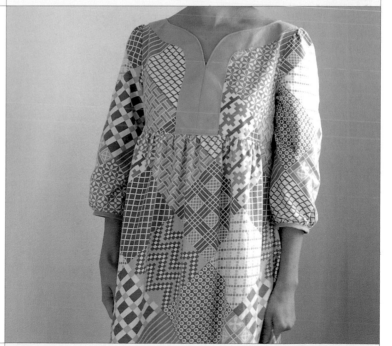

0292 EMU IZAKI, NEW ZEALAND

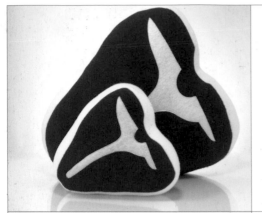

0293   LAUREN VENELL,
SWEET MEATS, USA

0294   ANNIKA GINSBERG,
MAHKA CRAFT, USA

0295   POUCH, UK

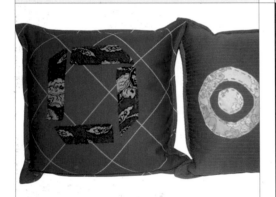

0296   KATE BINGAMAN-BURT, USA

0297   SUSAN CARLSON SKALAK, USA

0298   POUCH, UK

0299   DAVID CRAFT,
GOGREENCRAFT, USA

0300   PRIYA MANI, DENMARK

0301   JULEE DUNEKACKE JAEGER, USA

0302 GGRIPPO, TRASH-À-PORTER, USA

0303 STIKSEL, THE NETHERLANDS

0304 KATE BINGAMAN-BURT, USA

PHOTO BY SONYA REYNOLDS

0305 HEATHER BAIN, CANADA

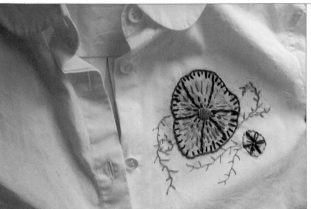

0306 JENNY HART, USA

0307 KAT BOWES,
THISTLEDOWN & FINCH, USA

0308 JOSIE MARSH, WOOLY BABY, USA

0309 JOSIE MARSH, WOOLY BABY, USA

0310 ROBYN L. COBURN,
IGGY JINGLES CRAFTS, USA

0311 KAT BOWES,
THISTLEDOWN & FINCH, USA

0312 ALISON LAIT, CANADA

0313 ASHLEY MARKUS,
OFF THE HOOKS, CANADA

0314   GGRIPPO, TRASH-À-PORTER, USA

jewelry+
adornments

0315–0523

0315 CARY ANN GRIMM, STUDIO (RE), USA

0316 CYNTHIA MURRAY DESIGN, USA

0317 LAUREN BEAUDOIN, CREATIVE DEXTERITY, USA

0318 FRANCESCA VITALI, USA

0319 KELLY WAKEFIELD-BEYTIA, USA

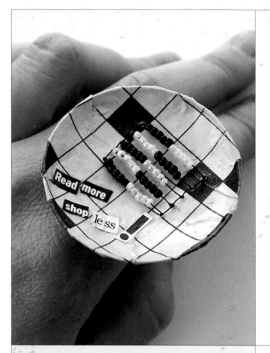

0320 **MIRAY ATACONLI, LILUMI, TURKEY**

0321 **DAUVIT ALEXANDER, UK**

0322 **LAUREN DONNELLY, PAPERELLE, USA**

0323 **JULIET AMES, THE BROKEN PLATE PENDANT CO., USA**

0324 **CHRISTINE DHEIN, USA**

0325 AIRDRIE MAKIM, AUSTRALIA

0326 ROMY SAI ZUNDE, INSECTUS ARTEFACTS, AUSTRALIA

0327 CHRISTINE DHEIN, USA

0328 DUSTIN WOOD, HANGER3, USA

0329 DUSTIN WOOD, HANGER3, USA

0330 SONYA COULSON ROOK, USA

0331 WARD WALLAU, TOKENS & ICONS, USA

0332 DUSTIN WOOD, HANGER3, USA

0333   JEN RODER, ROTORCAPS, USA

0334   ROMY SAI ZUNDE, INSECTUS ARTEFACTS, AUSTRALIA

0335   FRANCESCA VITALI, USA

0336   DAUVIT ALEXANDER, UK

0338 FRANCESCA VITALI, USA

0339   EDIE JOANNA OVERTURF, USA

0340   BETSY SIBOR, FOXGLOVE ACCESSORIES, USA

0341   VALERIE WILLIAM, ADDITIONS, USA

0342   AMALIA VERSACI, USA

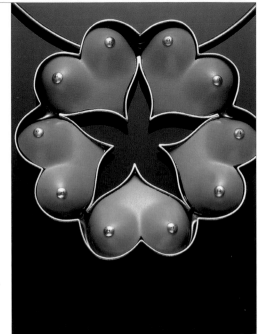

0343 MARGAUX LANGE, USA

0344 MARGAUX LANGE, USA

0345 MARGAUX LANGE, USA

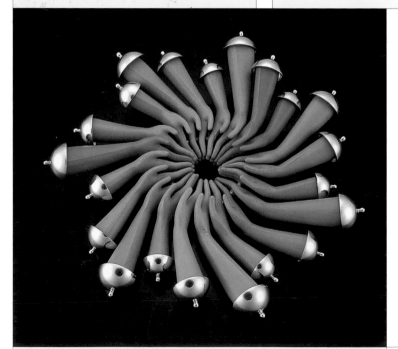

0346 MARGAUX LANGE, USA

0347 MARGAUX LANGE, USA

0348 MARGAUX LANGE, USA

0349 TERESA SULLIVAN, USA

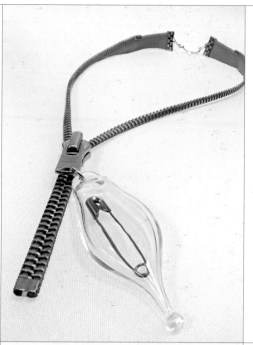

0350   JOYANN FLOWERS,
JOYA JEWELRY, USA

PHOTO BY A. JOHN TINHOLT

0351   VANESSA YANOW, CANADA

0352   BETSY SIBOR,
FOXGLOVE ACCESSORIES, USA

0353   EDIE JOANNA OVERTURF, USA

0354   RENEE DE SIBOUR, MY UGLY KITTY, USA

0355 JOYANN FLOWERS, JOYA JEWELRY, USA

0356 JEN RODER, ROTORCAPS, USA

0357 ALINA GRIDLEY, SILVER GARDEN, USA

0358 MISTY DARRINGTON, GEMMABEADS, USA

0359 JEANNETTE GUTIERREZ, USA

0360 JULIET AMES, THE BROKEN PLATE PENDANT CO., USA

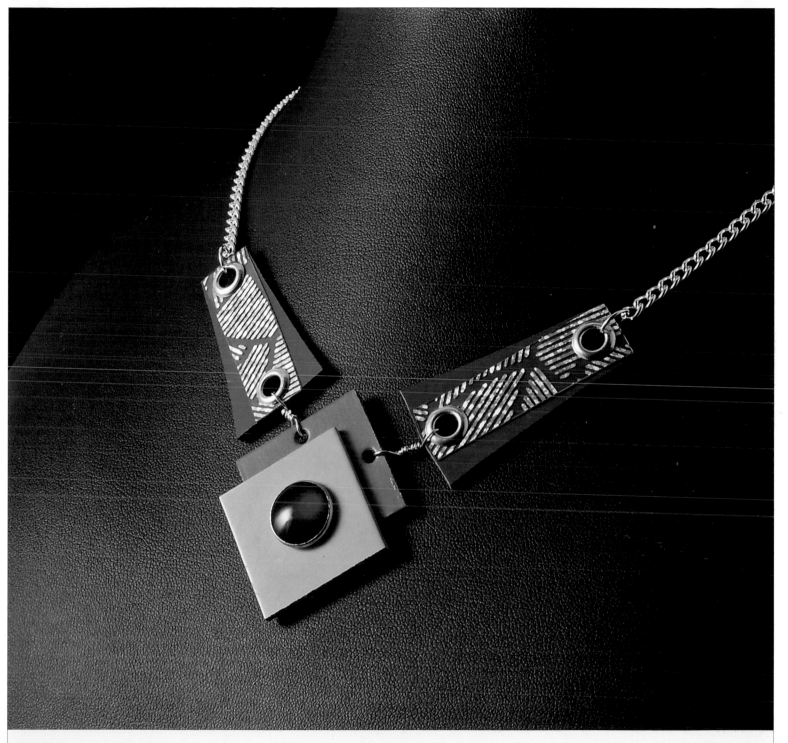

0362 KIM DEPENBROK, KD DESIGN STUDIO, USA

0363 SPOONERZ, USA

0364 LAUREN BALDWIN, USA

0365 FRANCESCA VITALI, USA

PHOTO BY GEORGE POST PHOTOGRAPHY

0366 WARD WALLAU, TOKENS & ICONS, USA

0367 SANDRA SALAMONY, USA

0368 REBECCA WARD, AUSTRALIA

0369 JESSIE DRISCOLL,
MADE FROM COINS, USA

0370 GI AND PINDO, USA

0371 PAMELA BURNS, ETCETRIX, USA

0372 ROBYN SPRUNG, USA

0373 SANDRA SALAMONY, USA

0374 VALERIE WILLIAM,
ADDITIONS, USA

0375 VALERIE WILLIAM, ADDITIONS, USA

0376 JESSIE DRISCOLL, MADE FROM COINS, USA

0377 JESSIE DRISCOLL, MADE FROM COINS, USA

0378 SONYA COULSON ROOK, USA

0379 SONYA COULSON ROOK, USA

0380 GUSTAV REYES, SIMPLY WOOD RINGS, USA

0381 GUSTAV REYES, SIMPLY WOOD RINGS, USA

0382 GUSTAV REYES, SIMPLY WOOD RINGS, USA

0383 CINDY CORDERO-STOUT, UK

0384 WARD WALLAU, TOKENS & ICONS, USA

0385 SONYA COULSON ROOK, USA

0386 GUSTAV REYES, SIMPLY WOOD RINGS, USA

0387 SHAWN TAYLOR, PRASSEIN DESIGN STUDIO, USA

0388 MARY-JO PERITORE, MERCURIOS, USA

0389 MISTY DARRINGTON, GEMMABEADS, USA

0390 SHAWN TAYLOR, PRASSEIN DESIGN STUDIO, USA

0391 SHAWN TAYLOR, PRASSEIN DESIGN STUDIO, USA

0392 BETH TODD, USA

0393 BRIAN WESTERN, WESTERN ART GLASS, USA

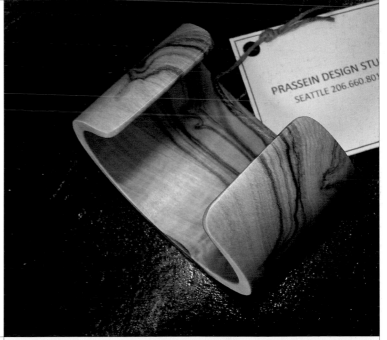

0394 SHAWN TAYLOR, PRASSEIN DESIGN STUDIO, USA

0395 JEN RODER, ROTORCAPS, USA

0396 MARIA CASTRILLO, SPAIN

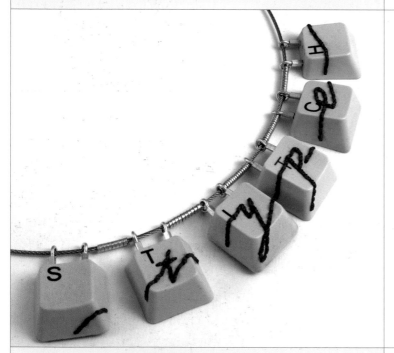

0397 REBECCA WARD, AUSTRALIA

0398 ETTI & OTTI'S ODDMENTS BY MICHELLE BISCOTTI, USA

0399 TAMMY GAY, CANADA

0400 CHRISTINE TERRELL, ADAPTIVE REUSE, USA

0401 WARD WALLAU, TOKENS & ICONS, USA

0402 MIRAY ATACONLI, LILUMI, TURKEY

0403 REBECCA WARD, AUSTRALIA

0404 DANIELLE HOLKE, CANADA

0405 2REVERT, CANADA

0406 NANCY SMYTHE THOMPSON, USA

0407 REBECCA WARD, AUSTRALIA

JEWELRY + ADORNMENTS

129

0408 JEANÉE LEDOUX, HONEYDOUX, USA

0409 SPOONERZ, USA

0410 AMALIA VERSACI, USA

0411 DAUVIT ALEXANDER, UK

0412 MICHELLE HARTNEY, RECYCLED RINGS, USA

0413 BETSY SIBOR, FOXGLOVE ACCESSORIES, USA

0414 TIFFANY TESKE, CANADA

PHOTO BY RALPH GABRINER

0415 STEVIE B., USA

0416 DANA DAMM, THOMASINA JEWELRY, USA

0417 DANIELLE HOLKE, CANADA

0418 REBECCA WARD, AUSTRALIA

0419 CYNTHIA WILLIAMS, USA

0420 PATRIZIA IACINO, GLOBALCOOLO JEWELRY, USA

PHOTO BY PHILIP COHEN

0421 HARRIETE ESTEL BERMAN, USA

0422 CHERY HOLMES, CANADA

0424 PATRIZIA IACINO, GLOBALCOOLO JEWELRY, USA

0425 VANESSA YANOW, CANADA

0426 KRISTIN LORA, USA

0427 IRIS MISHLY POLYMER CLAY ART, ISRAEL

0428 GI AND PINDO, USA

0429 GUYLAINE AND ISABELLE MARTINEAU,
.TOMATE D'ÉPINGLES, CANADA

0430 GI AND PINDO, USA

0431 GEGE KINGSTON, USA

0432 2REVERT, CANADA

0433 JULIET AMES, THE BROKEN PLATE PENDANT CO., USA

PHOTO BY GEORGE POST PHOTOGRAPHY

0434 WARD WALLAU, TOKENS & ICONS, USA

0435 MARGAUX KENT, THE BLACK SPOT BOOKS, USA

0436 JAMI GIGOT & NICOLAS WORTH,
THE GRATEFUL THREAD LTD., UK

PHOTO BY DON FELTON

0437 CHRISTINE DHEIN, USA

0438 TIFFANY TESKE, CANADA

0439 MONICA TOPPING, ROCK CHICK DESIGNS, USA

0440 OUTSAPOP TRASHION, FINLAND

0441 1MIND1, HUNGARY

0442 CHRISTINE CLARINGBOLD, EYE POP ART, USA

0443 MARIA CASTRILLO, SPAIN

0444 MONICA TOPPING, ROCK CHICK DESIGNS, USA

0445 LINDA AND OPIE O'BRIEN, USA

0446 GAYE MEDBURY, USA

0447 MISTY DARRINGTON, GEMMABEADS, USA

0448 ROMY SAI ZUNDE, INSECTUS ARTEFACTS, AUSTRALIA

0449 MARY-JO PERITORE, MERCURIOS, USA

0450 SPOONERZ, USA

0451 GAYE MEDBURY, USA

0452 ROBYN SPRUNG, USA

0453 DANIELLE HOLKE, CANADA

0454 FRANCESCA VITALI, USA

0455 CHERY HOLMES, CANADA

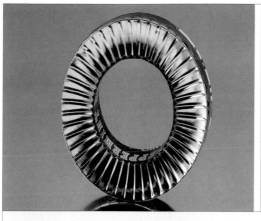

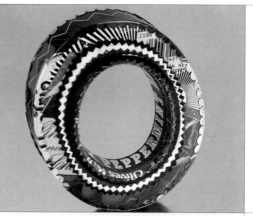

0456 HARRIETE ESTEL BERMAN, USA

0457 MIRAY ATACONLI, LILUMI, TURKEY

0458 BETH TODD, USA

0459 MICHELLE HARTNEY, RECYCLED RINGS, USA

0460 CHRISTINE TERRELL, ADAPTIVE REUSE, USA

0461 2REVERT, CANADA

0462 BETH TODD, USA

0463 CHERY HOLMES, CANADA

0464 CINDY CORDERO-STOUT, UK

0465 AMUCK, USA

0466 VALERIE WILLIAM, ADDITIONS, USA

0467 PAMELA BURNS, ETCETRIX, USA

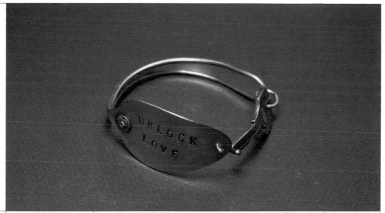

0469 HOLLY PRIESTER, BLUE FISH MOON STUDIOS, USA

0468 AMUCK, USA

0470 HOLLY PRIESTER, BLUE FISH MOON STUDIOS, USA

0471 AMUCK, USA

PHOTO BY A. JOHN TINHOLT

0472 VANESSA YANOW, CANADA

0473 CYNTHIA WILLIAMS, USA

0474 TAMMY GAY, CANADA

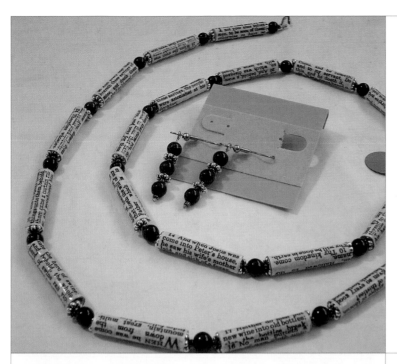

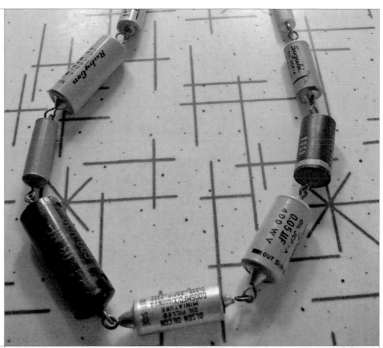

0475 BRENDA B. WRIGHT, BOWENWRIGHT CRAFTS, LC, USA

0476 DANA DAMM, THOMASINA JEWELRY, USA

0477 ROMY SAI ZUNDE, INSECTUS ARTEFACTS, AUSTRALIA

0478 PAMELA BURNS, ETCETRIX, USA

0479   AIRDRIE MAKIM, AUSTRALIA

0480   BRENDA B. WRIGHT, BOWENWRIGHT CRAFTS, LC, USA

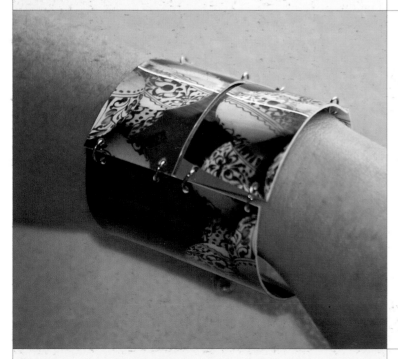

0481   TAMMY GAY, CANADA

0482   ROBYN SPRUNG, USA

0483 ROBYN SPRUNG, USA

0485 **MISTY DARRINGTON, GEMMABEADS, USA**

0486 **BECKY STERN, USA**

0484 **SYLVIA ANDERSON, USA**

0487 **ANNIE O'KANE, USA**

0488 **LIMOR YARON, PRODUCT DESIGNER, ISRAEL**

0489 **CHERY HOLMES, CANADA**

0490 CYNTHIA WILLIAMS, USA

0491 FRANCESCA VITALI, USA

0492 CHRISTINE CLARINGBOLD, EYE POP ART, USA

0493 TERESA SULLIVAN, USA

0494 KELLY BASINGER, USA

0495 JESSI C. WELCH, CHEAP DATE JEWELRY, USA

0496 LAUREN DONNELLY, PAPERELLE, USA

PHOTO BY HAP SAKWA

0497 KIRSTEN MUENSTER, USA

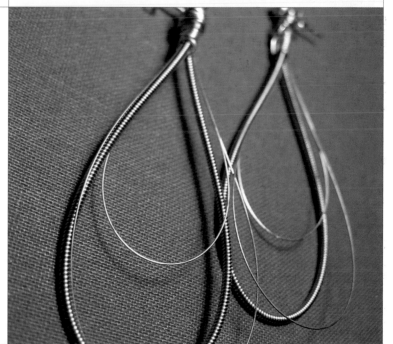

0498 JESSI C. WELCH, CHEAP DATE JEWELRY, USA

0499　ANNADA HYPES, TOKEN EMOTION, USA

0500　DIANE SCHAMP, USA

0501　MICHELLE HARTNEY, RECYCLED RINGS, USA

0502　ALICIA GOODWIN, USA

0503 JULIET AMES, THE BROKEN PLATE PENDANT CO., USA

0504 DANA DAMM, THOMASINA JEWELRY, USA

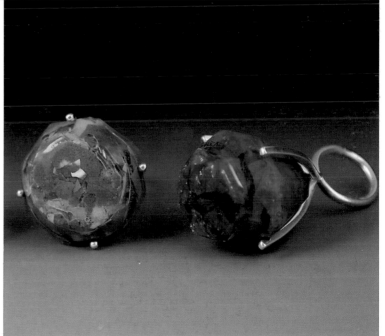

0505 JOYANN FLOWERS, JOYA JEWELRY, USA

0506 JENN PARNELL, SHERRI SHAWVER, USA

0507 NANCY SMYTHE THOMPSON, USA

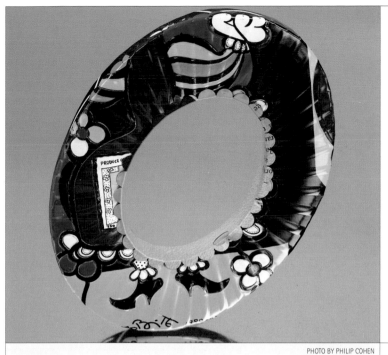

0508 HARRIETE ESTEL BERMAN, USA

0509 JEN RODER, ROTORCAPS, USA

0510 BRENDA B. WRIGHT, BOWENWRIGHT CRAFTS, LC, USA

0511 NANCY SMYTHE THOMPSON, USA

0512 LISA ORGLER DESIGN, USA

0513 DANIELLE HOLKE, CANADA

0514 EDIE JOANNA OVERTURF, USA

0515 ROBYN SPRUNG, USA

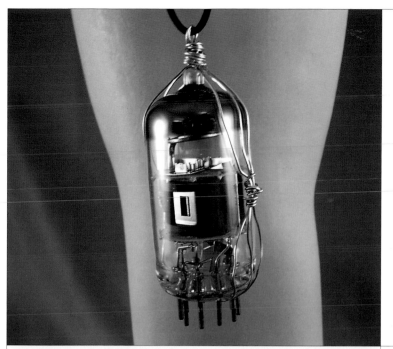

0516 MICHELE RAPPOPORT, BLINGALING, USA

0517 GEGE KINGSTON, USA

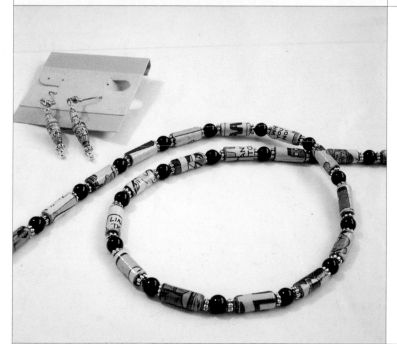

0518 BRENDA B. WRIGHT, BOWENWRIGHT CRAFTS, LC, USA

0519 JEANNETTE GUTIERREZ, USA

JEWELRY + ADORNMENTS

159

0520 1MIND1, HUNGARY

0521 DAUVIT ALEXANDER, UK

0522 PAMELA BURNS, ETCETRIX, USA

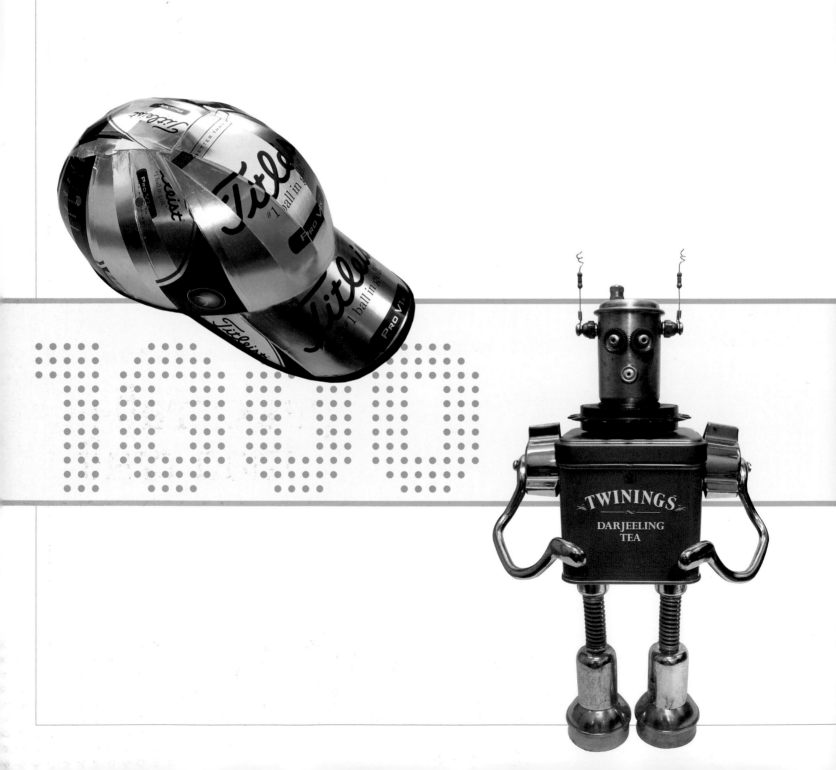

geek craft+
man craft

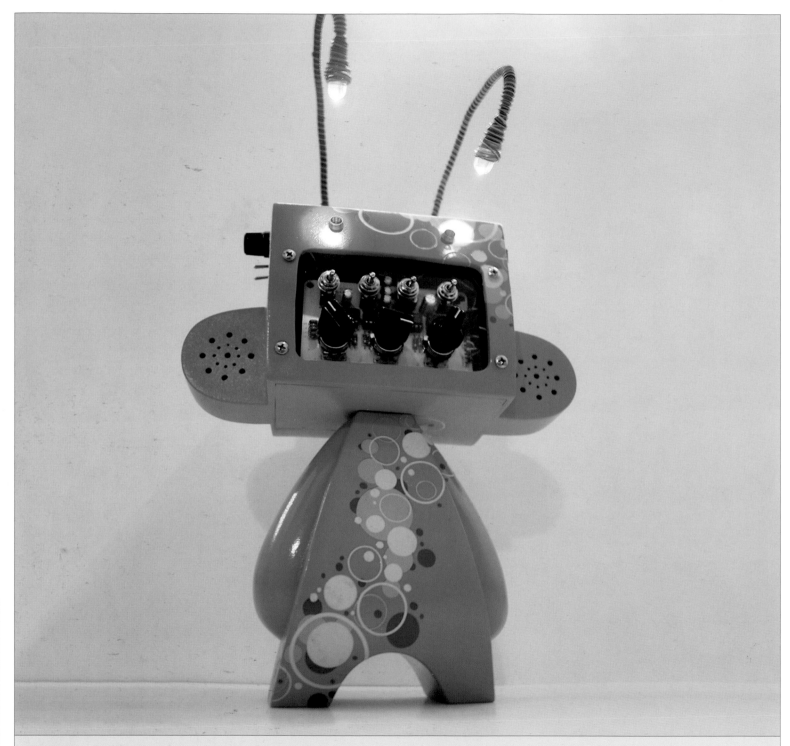

0524 DUSTIN CANTRELL, USA

0525 RYAN "ZIEAK" McFARLAND, USA

0526 NICHOLAS MARTIN PAUL, USA

0527 RYAN "ZIEAK" McFARLAND, USA

0528 RICHARD NAGY, DATAMANCER.NET, USA

0529 AMANDA PRESKE, USA

0530 AMANDA PRESKE, USA

0531 AMANDA PRESKE, USA

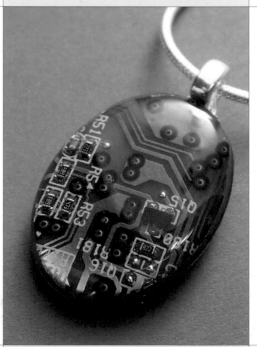

0532 AMANDA PRESKE, USA

0533 AMANDA PRESKE, USA

0534 AMANDA PRESKE, USA

0536 RICHARD NAGY, DATAMANCER.NET, USA

0537 KRISTIN LORA, USA

0538 JEFF JOHNSON, USA

0539 MATT PERRY, USA

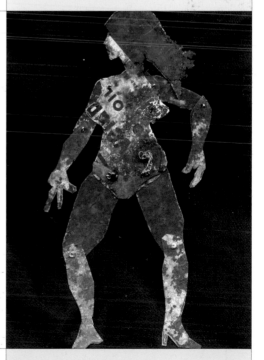

0540 NICHOLAS MARTIN PAUL, USA

0541 DAN JONES, TINKERBOTS, USA

0542 KEN FLETT, CANADA

0543   HENRY H. OWINGS, CHUNKLET GRAPHIC CONTROL, USA

0544   JESSE RUTHERFORD, BENT-TRONICS, USA

0545   LAUREN ANABELA BEAUDOIN, CREATIVE DEXTERITY, USA

0546   SEBASTIAN ZEHE, GERMANY

0547   LAUREN ANABELA BEAUDOIN, CREATIVE DEXTERITY, USA

0548   HENRY H. OWINGS, CHUNKLET GRAPHIC CONTROL, USA

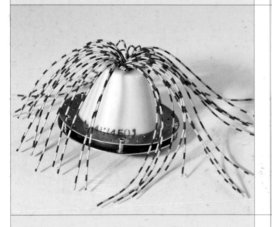

0549   KRISTIN LORA, USA

0550   HENRY H. OWINGS, CHUNKLET GRAPHIC CONTROL, USA

0551   LAUREN ANABELA BEAUDOIN, CREATIVE DEXTERITY, USA

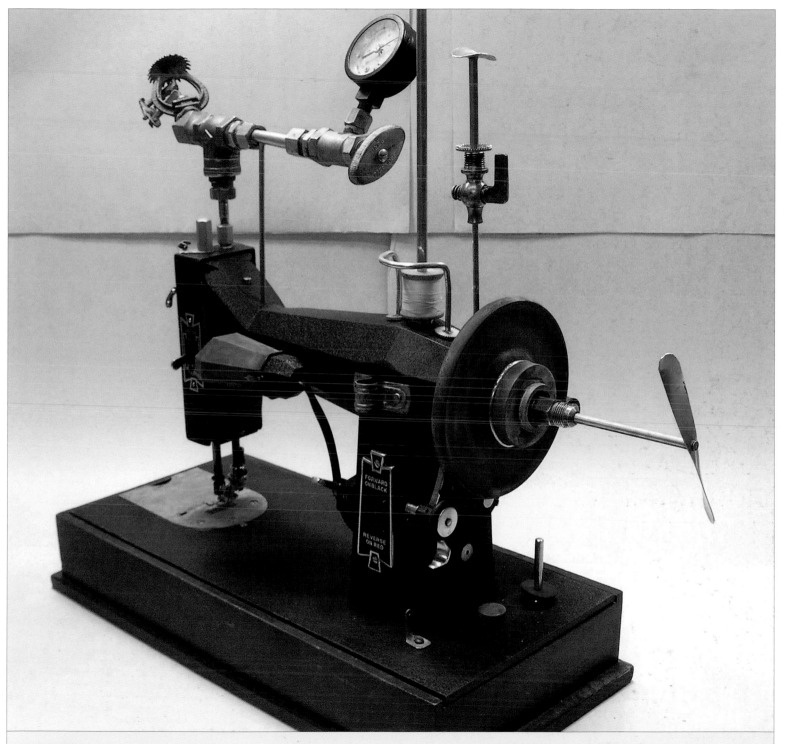

FORWARD
ON BLACK

REVERSE
ON RED

0553 JISKAR SCHMITZ, THE NETHERLANDS

0554 CURRAN ALEXANDER ARNETT, UK

0555 JISKAR SCHMITZ,
THE NETHERLANDS

0556 JULEE DUNEKACKE JAEGER, USA

0557 JULEE DUNEKACKE JAEGER, USA

0558 CURRAN ALEXANDER ARNETT, UK

0559 DAVID LIPSON,
LIPSON ROBOTICS, USA

0560 DUSTIN CANTRELL, USA

0561 DAVID LIPSON,
LIPSON ROBOTICS, USA

0562 DAN JONES, TINKERBOTS, USA

PHOTO BY MEGAN WAGNER

0563 JEREMY T. HOWARD, USA

0564 DAN JONES, USA

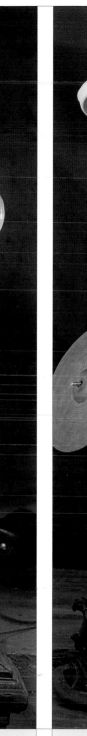

0565 ALAN LISHNESS, USA

0566 JEREMY T. HOWARD, USA

0567 DUSTIN CANTRELL, USA

0568 TOM KABAT, WOODENBIKES, USA

0569 DAN JONES, TINKERBOTS, USA

0570 RICHARD NAGY, DATAMANCER.NET, USA

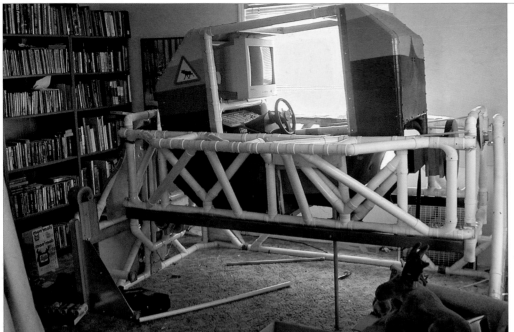

0571 SAM GUEYDON AND FRIENDS, USA

0572 JISKAR SCHMITZ,
THE NETHERLANDS

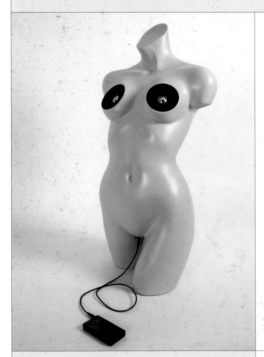

0573 BOB TUREK, USA

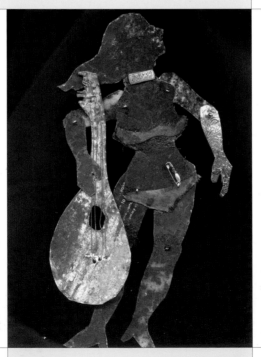

0574 KEN FLETT, CANADA

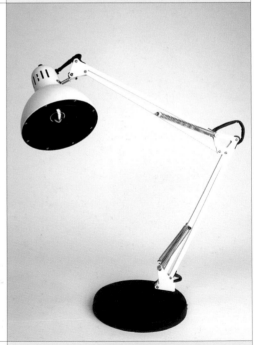

0575 BOB TUREK, USA

0576 TOM KABAT, WOODENBIKES, USA

0577 JOHN T. UNGER, USA

0578 JESSE RUTHERFORD, BENT-TRONICS, USA

0579 MATT JOYCE, NYCRESISTOR, USA

0580 STEVE TRAVIS, USA

1000 IDEAS FOR CREATIVE REUSE

0581 JOHN T. UNGER, USA

0582 TOM KABAT, WOODENBIKES, USA

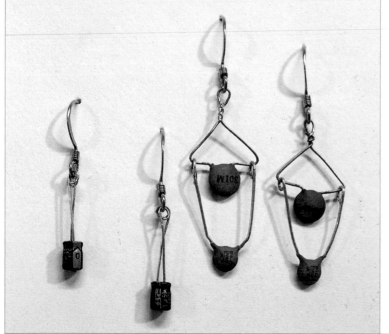

0583 BECKY STERN, USA

0584 DAN JONES, TINKERBOTS, USA

0585 DAN JONES, TINKERBOTS, USA

0586 DAVID CRAFT, GOGREENCRAFT, USA

0587 DAVID CRAFT, GOGREENCRAFT, USA

0588 MATT PERRY, USA

0589   MATT PERRY, USA

0590   DAVID CRAFT, GOGREENCRAFT, USA

0591   DAVID CRAFT, GOGREENCRAFT, USA

0592   IAIN McCAIG, UK

0595 BECKY STERN, USA

0593 CHRISTINE DHEIN, USA

0594 DUSTIN CANTRELL, USA

0596 JULEE DUNEKACKE JAEGER, USA

0597 KRISTIN LORA, USA

0598 DAVID LIPSON, LIPSON ROBOTICS, USA

0599 KRISTIN LORA, USA

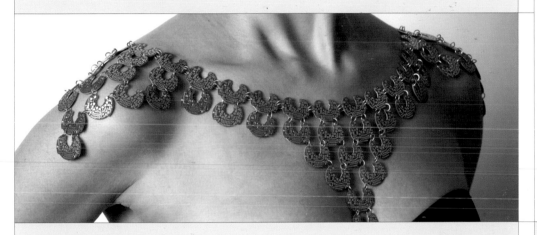

0600 CHRISTINE DHEIN, USA

0601 DAVID LIPSON,
       LIPSON ROBOTICS, USA

0602 LAUREN ANABELA BEAUDOIN,
       CREATIVE DEXTERITY, USA

0603 RENE KREIS, USA

0604 HENRY H. OWINGS,
       CHUNKLET GRAPHIC CONTROL, USA

0605 IAN BROWN, AUSTRALIA

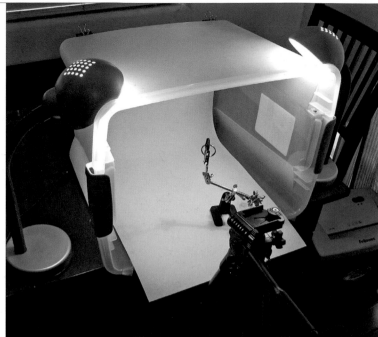

0606 JESSE RUTHERFORD, BENT-TRONICS, USA

0607 ANDRES SAVI, ESTONIA

0608 SEBASTIAN ZEHE, GERMANY

0609 RICHARD NAGY, DATAMANCER.NET, USA

0610 RICHARD NAGY, DATAMANCER.NET, USA

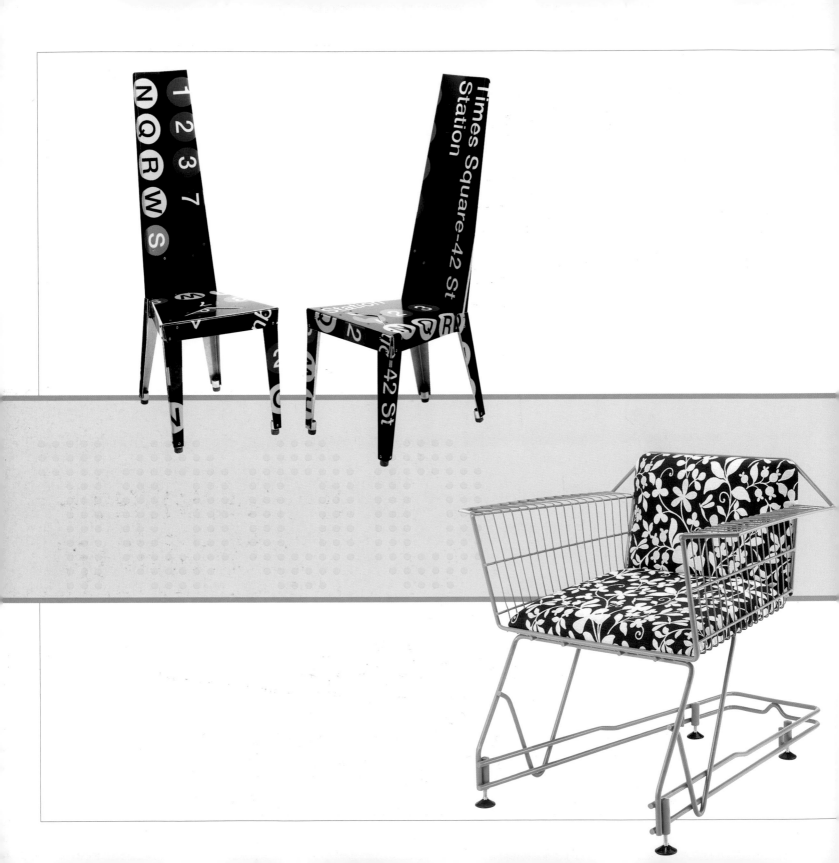

housewares+
furnishings

0611–0830

0611   WILL HUNT, AUSTRALIA

0612 MICHELLE KAUFMANN, USA

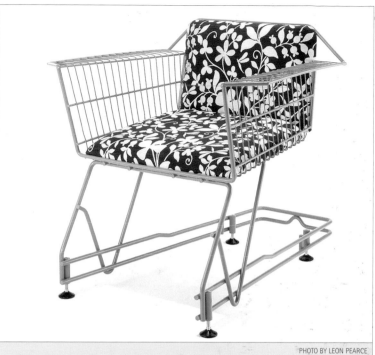

0613 REESTORE LTD., UK

0614 WHIT MCLEOD FURNITURE, USA

0615 WALTER KENT, THE BLACK SPOT BOOKS, USA

0616 REESTORE LTD., UK

0617 LIZ DICKEY, 1.BY.LIZ, USA

0618 ATYPYK, FRANCE

0619 SARAH OLMSTEAD, USA

1000 IDEAS FOR CREATIVE REUSE

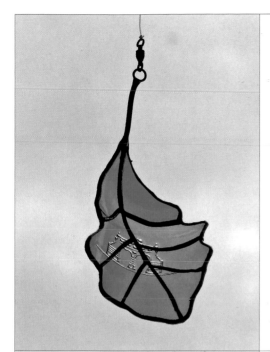

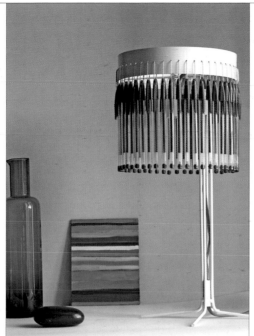

0620 BRIAN WESTERN, WESTERN ART GLASS, USA

0621 LUCAN MUÑOZ AND DAVID TAMAME, ENPIENZA! ESTUDIO, SPAIN

0622 MITCHELL GLASSWORKS, USA

PHOTO BY ANJA SJÖGREN

0623 CLAY McLAURIN, USA

0624 CLAY McLAURIN, USA

0625 DESIGN STORIES, SWEDEN

0626 HEATHER GOLDBERG, USA

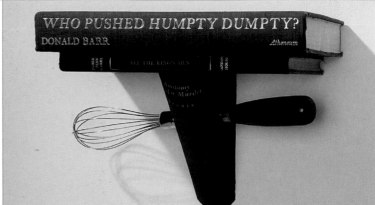

WHO PUSHED HUMPTY DUMPTY?
DONALD BARR   Atheneum

0627 JIM ROSENAU, USA

0628 RUNA LEO AND JON MARÍN, SPAIN

0629 LIZ DICKEY, 1.BY.LIZ, USA

0630 JIM ROSENAU, USA

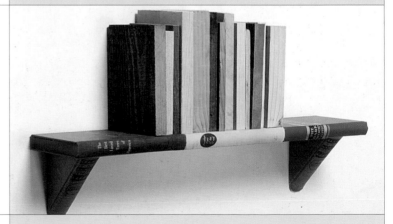

0631 JIM ROSENAU, USA

0633 JOHN HARDIN, TIN CAN LUMINARY, USA

0632 ADAM PATRICK EASTER COTTINGHAM, USA

0634 HOLLAND SEYDEL AND ELIAV NISSAN, HAUTE NATURE, USA

0636 KIM TAYLOR, THE SASSY CRAFTER, USA

0637 KIM TAYLOR, THE SASSY CRAFTER, USA

0638 SUSAN BEAL, USA

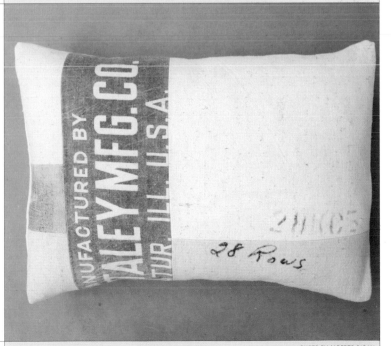

0639 REBECCA TEGTMEYER, SOWN DESIGNS, USA

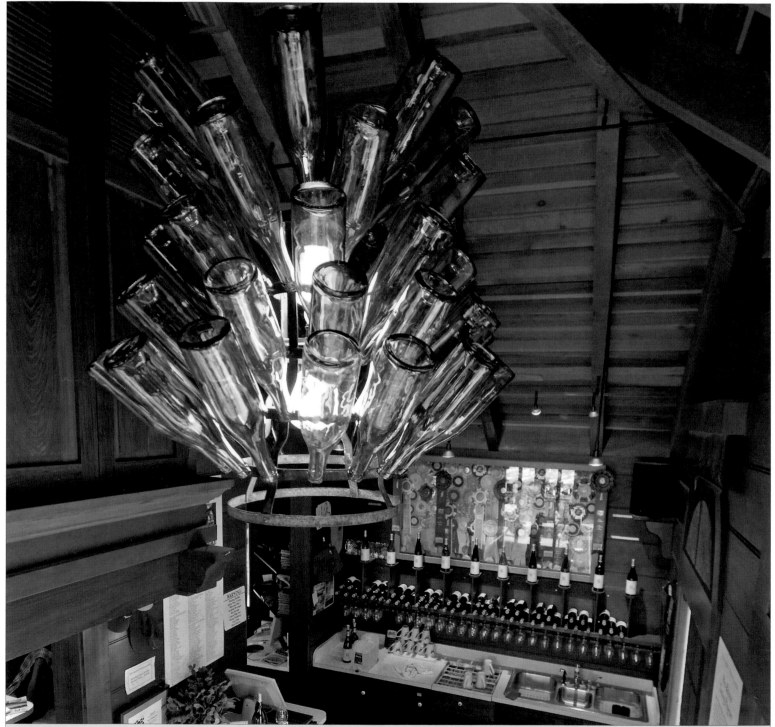

0640   NAVARRO VINEYARDS, USA

0641 JULIET HEIL,
GREENER LANDZ, USA

PHOTO BY JENNIFER FIERO

0642 HEATHER GOLDBERG, USA

0643 AMY M. SANTOFERRARO, USA

0644 JOHN HARDIN, TIN CAN LUMINARY, USA

0645 BREE NORLANDER,
HOT TEA APPAREL, USA

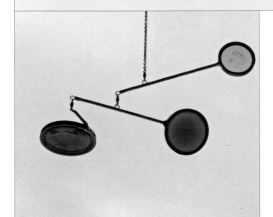

0646 BRIAN WESTERN,
WESTERN ART GLASS, USA

0647 SUSAN BEAL, USA

0648 MICHELLE KAUFMANN, USA

0649 CHRISTINE CLARINGBOLD, EYE POP ART, USA

0650 SUSAN BEAL, USA

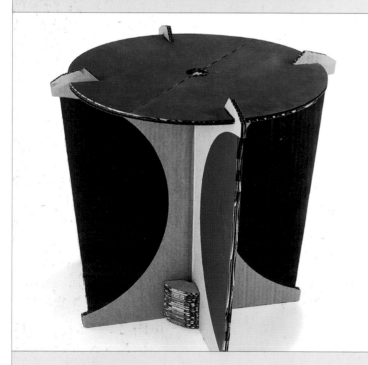

0651 IAN GONSHER, USA

0652 JEFF DAVIS, VINYLUX, USA

0653 BRIAN PETERS & DAPHNE FIROS, USA

0654 CHRISTINE CLARINGBOLD, EYE POP ART, USA

0655 LUCAS MUÑOZ AND DAVID TAMANE, ENPIEZA! ESTUDIO, SPAIN

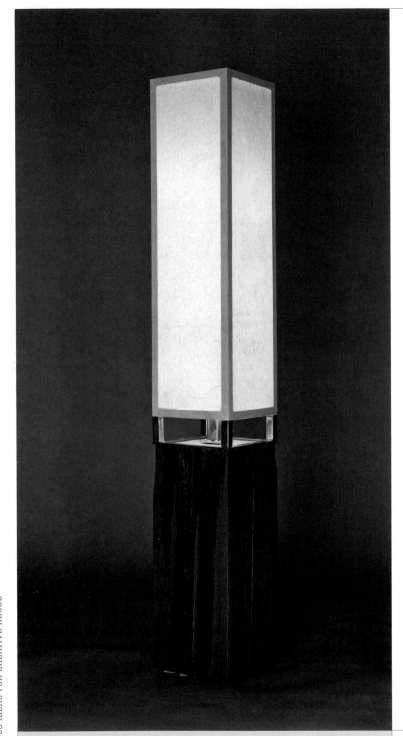

0656 RANDALL KRAMER, USA

0657 RANDALL KRAMER, USA

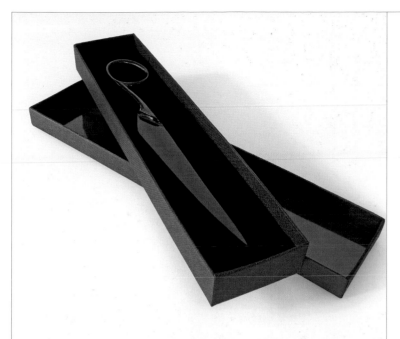

0658 ATYPYK, FRANCE

0659 TIFFANY TESKE, CANADA

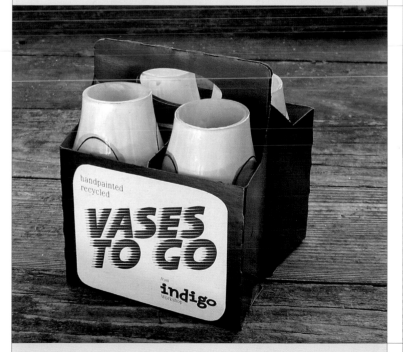

handpainted
recycled

VASES
TO GO

from
indigo
Workshop

0660 JANN GREENLAND, USA

0661 TIFFANY TESKE, CANADA

0662 STUDIO CHERIE, USA

0663 BECKY STERN, USA

0664 KIM TAYLOR, THE SASSY CRAFTER, USA

PHOTO BY DONALD MALUMPHY

0665 ALICE TRUMBULL, USA

0666 MAGGIE FRENCH, USA

0667 HEYBALES, USA

0668 RANDALL CLEAVER, USA

0669 KIM TAYLOR,
THE SASSY CRAFTER, USA

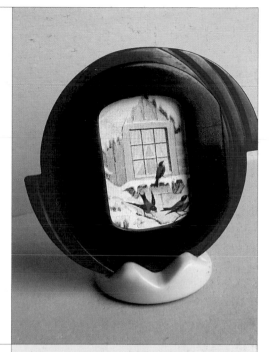

0670 HEATHER GOLDBERG, USA

0671 IDOLLY SCHWENDENER, CANADA

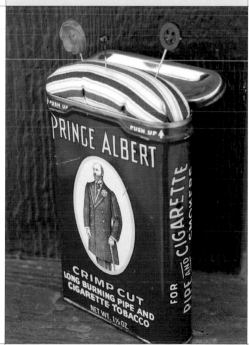

0672 TERESA JESSEE,
2BIRDS1STONE, USA

PHOTO BY JENNIFER FIERO

0673 JULIET HEIL,
GREENER LANDZ, USA

0674 RANDALL KRAMER, USA

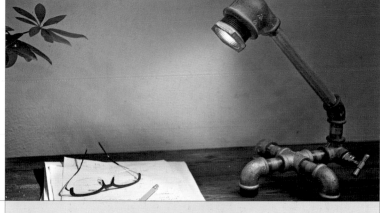

0675 JOHN HARDIN, TIN CAN LUMINARY, USA

0676 DAVID BENATAN, KOZO LAMPS, ISRAEL

PHOTO BY AARON KRAMER

PHOTO BY ANJA SJÖGREN

0677 AARON KRAMER, URBAN OBJECTS, USA

0678 DESIGN STORIES, SWEDEN

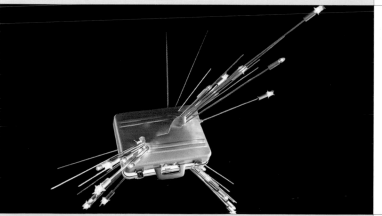

0679 TED SWIET, USA

0680 DUSTIN WOOD, HANGER3, USA

0681 BORIS BALLY, USA

0682 CHRISTINE FARNAN, USA

PHOTO BY AARON KRAMER

0683 AARON KRAMER, URBAN OBJECTS, USA

0684 ELIZABETH LUNDBERG MORISETTE, USA

0685 ANDREA SCHNEEBERG, USA

PHOTO BY ALBERTO RIGAU

0686 REBECCA TEGTMEYER, SOWN DESIGNS, USA

0687 CHICA AND JO, USA

0688 JEFF DAVIS, VINYLUX, USA

0689 HEATHER GOLDBERG, USA

0692 ALICIA L. WOODS, USA

0693 NICHOLAS MARTIN PAUL, USA

0694 LAURA CAHILL, UK

0695 MEGAN KLEPP, TA-DAH, USA

0696 JEFF ALEXANDER, JALEX STUDIOS, USA

0697 JEFF ALEXANDER, JALEX STUDIOS, USA

0698 RANDALL KRAMER, USA

0699 BORIS BALLY, USA

0700 BORIS BALLY, USA

PHOTO BY GEORGE POST PHOTOGRAPHY

0701 WARD WALLAU, BORIS BALLY, GRAHAM BERGH, USA

0702 BORIS BALLY, USA

0703   CHRISTIE CHASE, USA

0704 RANDALL CLEAVER, USA

0705 GIL DELAPOINTE, PIERRE ANDRE SENIZERGUES, USA

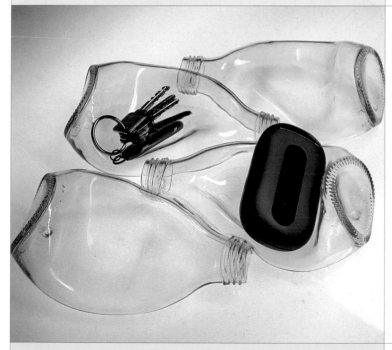

0706 BRYAN NORTHRUP, USA

0707 JOHN HARDIN, TIN CAN LUMINARY, USA

0708 AARON KRAMER,
URBAN OBJECTS, USA

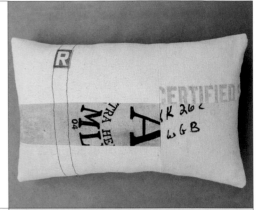

0709 REBECCA TEGTMEYER,
SOWN DESIGNS, USA

0710 TIFFANY THREADGOULD,
REPLAYGROUND, USA

0711 AMANDA SISKA,
BREAD AND BADGER, USA

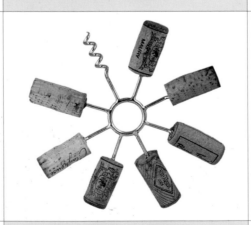

0712 HOLLAND SEYDEL AND ELIAV
NISSAN, HAUTE NATURE, USA

0713 TIFFANY THREADGOULD,
REPLAYGROUND, USA

0714 LAURA CAHILL, UK

0715+0716 LAURA CAHILL, UK

0717 RYAN HABBYSHAW, USA

0718 COLLEEN MARIA CASEY, USA

0719 COLLEEN MARIA CASEY, USA

0720 KIM TAYLOR, THE SASSY CRAFTER, USA

0721 SANDRA SALAMONY, USA

1000 IDEAS FOR CREATIVE REUSE

0722 COLLEEN MARIA CASEY, USA

0723 NANCY GAMON, USA

PHOTO BY STEVEN BROWN

0724 SARAH HAYES OWINGS, USA

0725 AMANDA SISKA, BREAD AND BADGER, USA

0726 BORIS BALLY, USA

0727 CHRISTINE CLARINGBOLD, EYE POP ART, USA

PHOTO BY DONALD MALUMPHY

0728 ALICE TRUMBULL, USA

0729 BORIS BALLY, USA

0730   DESIGN STORIES, SWEDEN

PHOTO BY ANJA SJÖGREN

0731   JAMI GIGOT AND NICOLAS WORTH, THE GRATEFUL THREAD LTD., UK

0732   VANDA SOUSA, PORTUGAL

0733   AMANDA SISKA, BREAD AND BADGER, USA

0734 TED SWIET, USA

0735 HEATHER BAIN, CANADA
PHOTO BY SONYA REYNOLDS

0736 AMANDA SISKA, BREAD AND BADGER, USA

0737 LUCAS MUÑOZ AND DAVID TAMANE, ENPIEZA! ESTUDIO, SPAIN

0738 JEFF ALEXANDER, JALEX STUDIOS, USA

0739 AMANDA SISKA, BREAD AND BADGER, USA

0740 TIFFANY THREADGOULD, REPLAYGROUND, USA

HOUSEWARES + FURNISHINGS

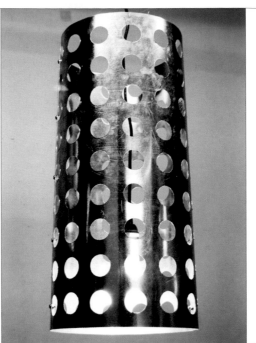

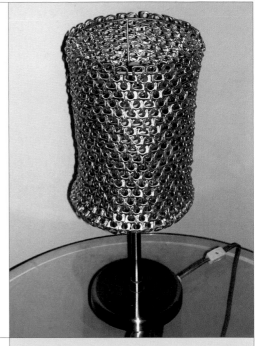

0741 WENDY UHLMAN, INDUSTRIAL DESIGNER, USA

0742 WENDY UHLMAN, INDUSTRIAL DESIGNER, USA

0743 SEAN MICHAEL RAGON, USA

0744 LIZ DICKEY, 1.BY.LIZ, USA

0745 LIZ DICKEY, 1.BY.LIZ, USA

0746 DAVID BENATAN, KOZO LAMPS, ISRAEL

0747 GRAHAM BERGH, UNCOMMON GOODS, USA

0748 CONSTANCE OLD, CO. INC., USA

0749 DAVID BENATAN, KOZO LAMPS, ISRAEL

0750 EMILY MACHOVEC, USA

0751   STEVEN SMITH, THABTO LTD., UK

0752   WHIT McLEOD FURNITURE, USA

0753   GIL DELAPOINTE AND PIERRE ANDRE SENIZERGUES, USA

0754   WHIT McLEOD FURNITURE, USA

0755 ERWIN TIMMERS, USA

0756 DESIGN STORIES, SWEDEN

0757 SEAN MICHAEL RAGAN, USA

0758 ANNADA HYPES, TOKEN EMOTION, USA

PHOTO BY ANJA SJÖGREN

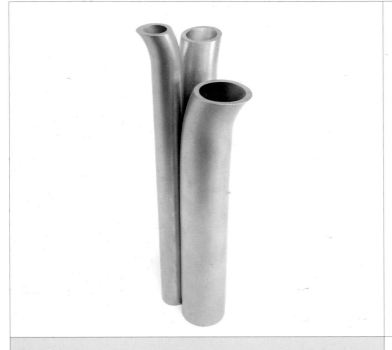

0760 LOOM STUDIO, USA

0761 CONSTANCE OLD, CO. INC., USA

0762 TIFFANY TESKE, CANADA

0763 TAYLOR CASS STEVENSON, USA

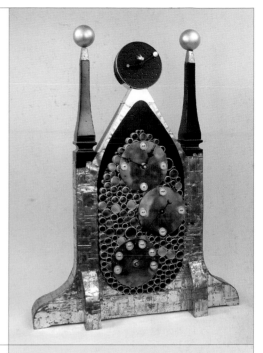

0764 JEFF ALEXANDER, JALEX STUDIOS, USA

0765 LUCAS MUÑOZ AND DAVID TAMAME, ENPIEZA! ESTUDIO, SPAIN

0766 RANDALL CLEAVER, USA

0767 JEANÉE LEDOUX, RE-CONSTRUCT DVD, USA

0768 IDOLLY SCHWENDENER, CANADA

0769 ERWIN TIMMERS, USA

0770 CONSTANCE OLD, CO. INC., USA

0771 AMANDA SISKA, BREAD AND BADGER, USA

0772 KATHERINE RASMUSSEN, REITER8, USA

1000 IDEAS FOR CREATIVE REUSE

0775 CAT MERRICK, USA

0776 AMANDA FIEDLER, USA

0777 CONSTANCE OLD, CO. INC., USA

0778 JANN GREENLAND, USA

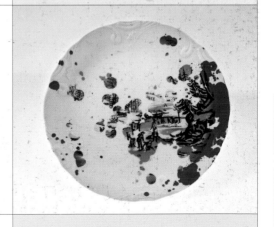

0779 LUCAS MUÑOZ AND DAVID TAMAME, ENPIEZA! ESTUDIO, SPAIN

0780 CAT MERRICK, USA

0781 CAT MERRICK, USA

0782   SARAH OLMSTEAD, USA

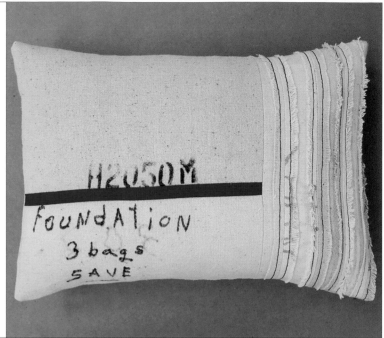

0783   REBECCA TEGTMEYER, SOWN DESIGNS, USA

0784   JANET HICKEY, USA

0785   GIL DELAPOINTE, PIERRE ANDRE SENIZERGUES, USA

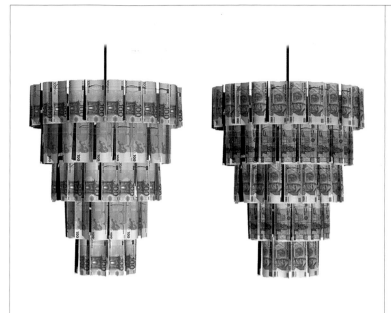

0786 STUART KARTEN DESIGN, USA

0787 AMALIA VERSACI, USA

0788 LIZ DICKEY, 1.BY.LIZ, USA

0789 ENGLISHCOOKIES, UK

0790 SUSAN BEAL, USA

0791 SUSAN BEAL, USA

0792 LIZ DICKEY, 1.BY.LIZ, USA

0793 KIM TAYLOR, THE SASSY CRAFTER, USA

0794 BETH TODD, USA

0795 ALICIA L. WOODS, USA

0796 RANDALL KRAMER, USA

0797 MICHELLE KAUFMANN, USA

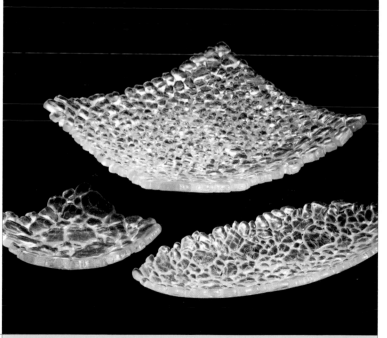

PHOTO BY ANYTHINGPHOTO.NET

0798 ERWIN TIMMERS, USA

0799 HEATHER BAIN, CANADA

PHOTO BY SONYA REYNOLDS

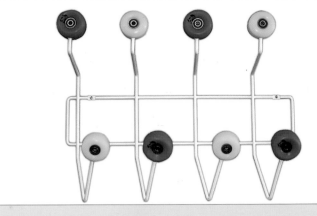

0800 GIL DELAPOINTE AND PIERRE ANDRE SENIZERGUES, USA

0801 BRYAN NORTHRUP, USA

0802 LAURA HAWKER PLOUZEK, XOELLE, USA

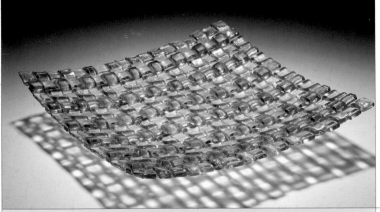

PHOTO BY ANYTHINGPHOTO.NET

0803 ERWIN TIMMERS, USA

0804 NICHOLAS MARTIN PAUL, USA

1000 IDEAS FOR CREATIVE REUSE

0805 TERRY AND MARY McCOY, INOUDID'S ATTIC, USA

0806 CHANDRA L. CORCORAN, USA

0807 LARA NEWSOM, HANDMADE PRETTIES, USA

0808 GIL DELAPOINTE AND PIERRE ANDRE SENIZERGUES, USA

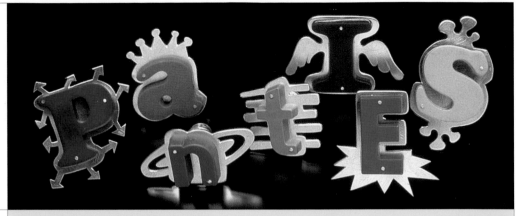

0809 BORIS BALLY, USA

0810 LAUREL NATHANSON, USA

0811 GGRIPPO, TRASH-À-PORTER, USA

0812 CHANDRA L. CORCORAN, USA

0813 JEFF DAVIS, VINYLUX, USA

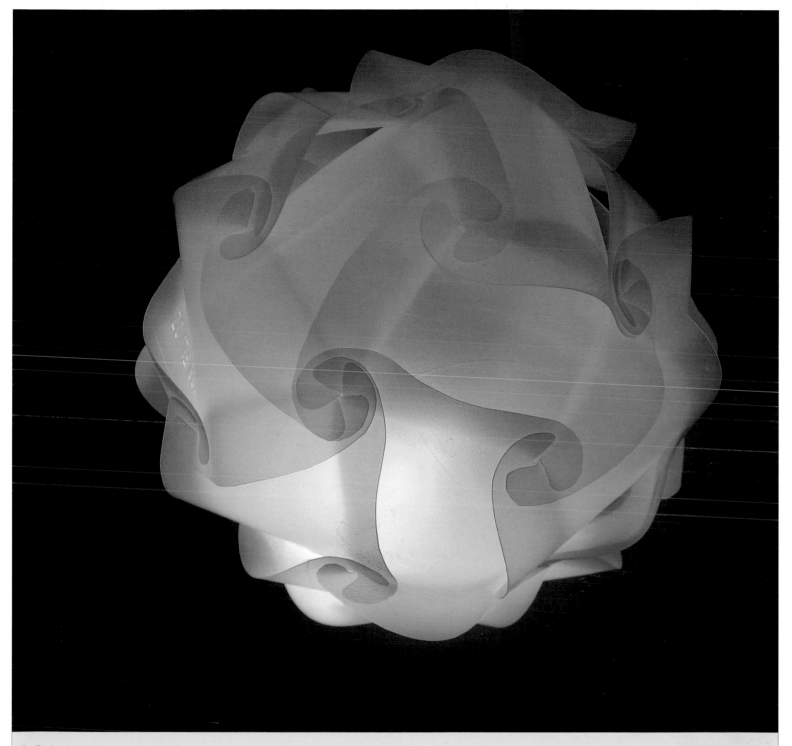

0814 KELLY BASINGER, USA

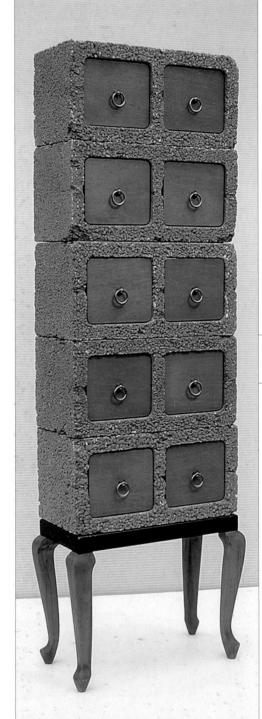

0815 GAYE MEDBURY, USA

0816 VANDA SOUSA, PORTUGAL

0817 AMI DRACH AND
DOV GANCHROW, ISRAEL

0818 JEFF ALEXANDER,
JALEX STUDIOS, USA

0819 MITCHELL GLASSWORKS, USA

0820 CLAY McLAURIN, USA

0821 AMI DRACH AND DOV GANCHROW, ISRAEL

0822 CLAY McLAURIN, USA

0823 RYAN "ZIEAK" MCFARLAND, USA

0824 ALANA BEALL, VANITY'S EDGE DESIGN, USA

0825 CLAY McLAURIN, USA

0826 AMI DRACH AND DOV GANCHROW, ISRAEL

0827 ANNEKE JAKOBS, THE NETHERLANDS

0828 AMI DRACH AND
DOV GANCHROW, ISRAEL

0829 LAURA HAWKER PLOUZEK, XOELLE, USA

0830 LARA NEWSOM, HANDMADE PRETTIES, USA

art, installations
+interiors

0831–1000

0831   THOMAS ALLEN, USA

0832 THOMAS ALLEN, USA

0833 THOMAS ALLEN, USA

0834 THOMAS ALLEN, USA

0835 THOMAS ALLEN, USA

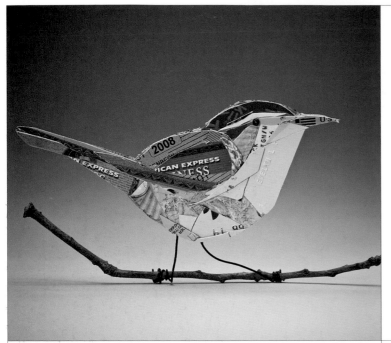

0836 BRYANT HOLSENBECK, USA

0837 BRYANT HOLSENBECK, USA

0838 BRYANT HOLSENBECK, USA

0839 BRYANT HOLSENBECK, USA

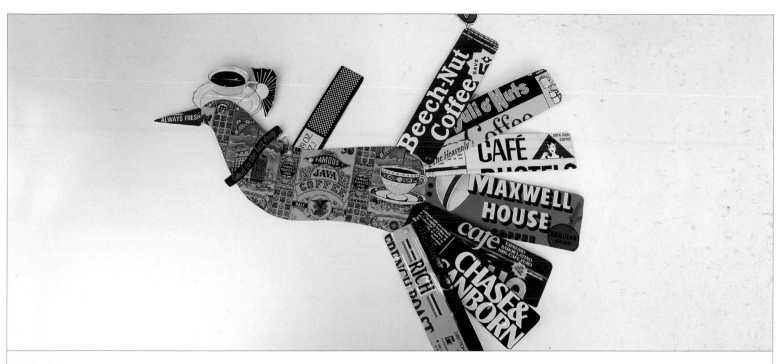

0840   SALLY SEAMANS, TIN CAN SALLY, USA

0841   SALLY SEAMANS, TIN CAN SALLY, USA

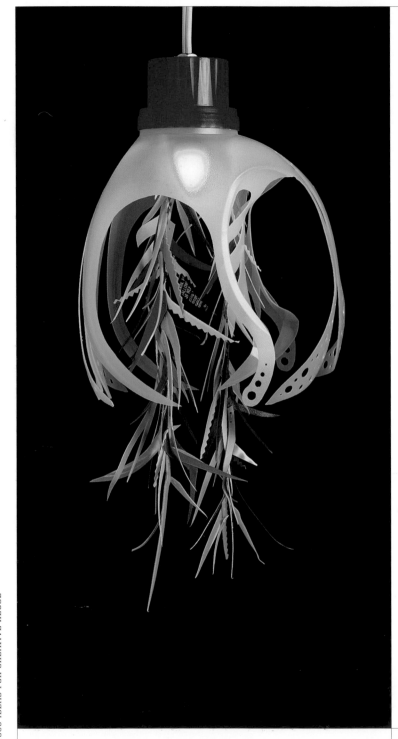

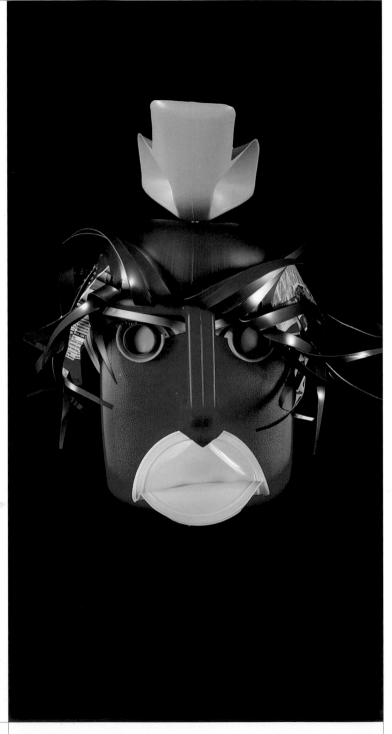

0842 DAVID EDGAR, PLASTIQUARIUM, USA

0843 DAVID EDGAR, PLASTIQUARIUM, USA

0844 DAVID EDGAR, PLASTIQUARIUM, USA

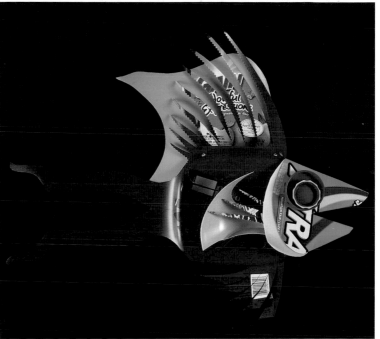

0845 DAVID EDGAR, PLASTIQUARIUM, USA

0846 DAVID EDGAR, PLASTIQUARIUM, USA

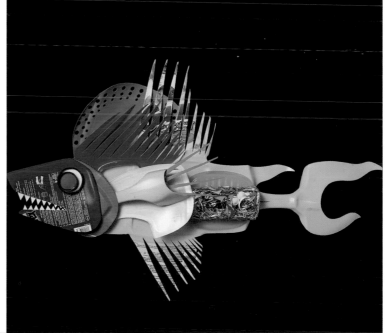

0847 DAVID EDGAR, PLASTIQUARIUM, USA

0848 WHITNEY LEE, USA

0849 WHITNEY LEE, USA

0850 WHITNEY LEE, USA

0851 WHITNEY LEE, USA

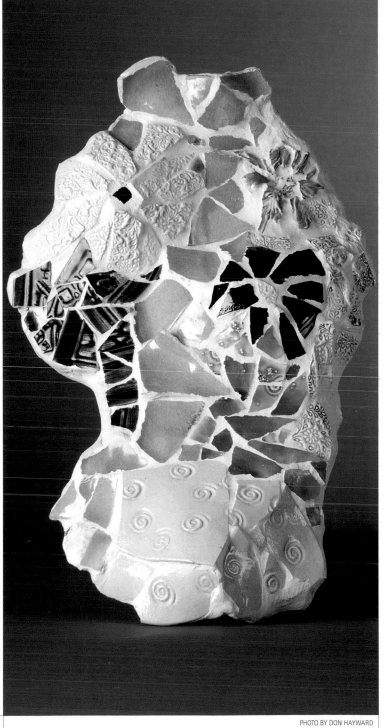

0852 WHITNEY LEE, USA

0853 JODIE ATHERTON, WHITEWATER CERAMICS, USA

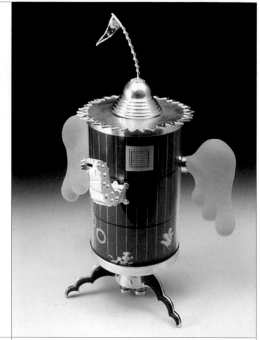

0854 TERESA SULLIVAN, USA

0855 TERESA SULLIVAN, USA

0856 LAUREL NATHANSON, USA

0857 LAUREL NATHANSON, USA

0858 THE CITYSTORYTELLERS, VERY SERIOUS URBAN STORYTELLING SOCIETY, THE NETHERLANDS

0859 JOSHUA BIENKO, USA

0860 PATTIE CHALMERS, USA

0861 PATTIE CHALMERS, USA

0862 PATTIE CHALMERS, USA

0863 PATTIE CHALMERS, USA

0864 PATTIE CHALMERS, USA

0865 JODIE ATHERTON, WHITEWATER CERAMICS, USA

0866 **JULIETTE MONTAGUE AND GREG STANGE, USA**

0867 **JULIETTE MONTAGUE AND GREG STANGE, USA**

0868 **KATHY TIBBETS, USA**

0869 **JULIETTE MONTAGUE AND GREG STANGE, USA**

0870 **JULIETTE MONTAGUE AND GREG STANGE, USA**

0871 **BEN SCHACHTER, USA**

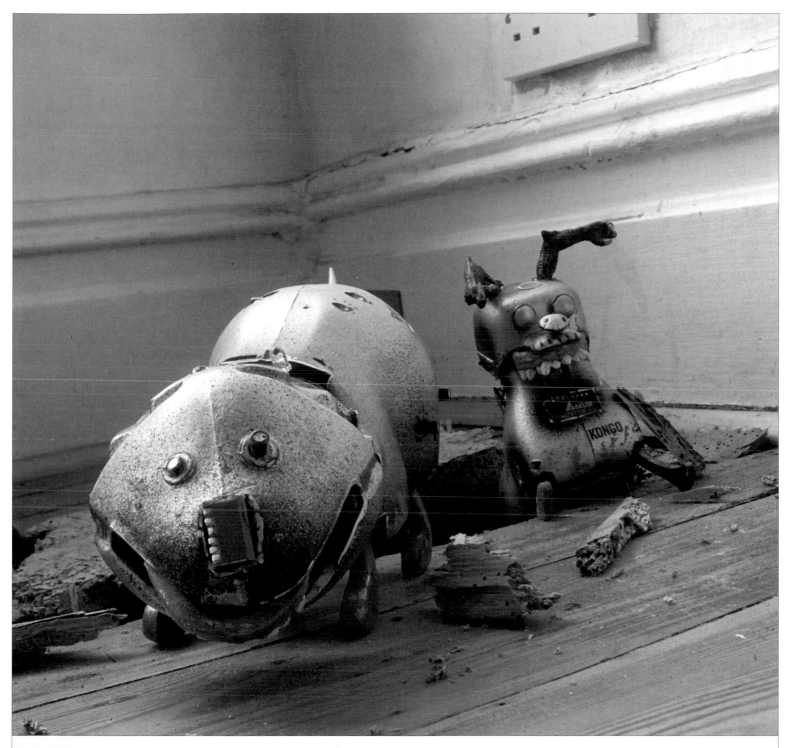

0872 MR. SPUNKY, UK

0873 RÜDIGER SCHLÖMER, GERMANY

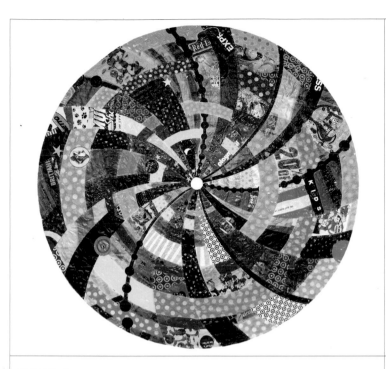

0874 VIRGINIA FLECK, USA

0875 VIRGINIA FLECK, USA

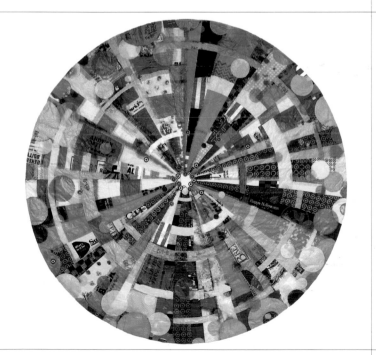

0876 VIRGINIA FLECK, USA

0877 VIRGINIA FLECK, USA

0878 HARRIETE ESTEL BERMAN, USA

0879 HARRIETE ESTEL BERMAN, USA

0880 HARRIETE ESTEL BERMAN, USA

0881 DIDI DUNPHY, USA

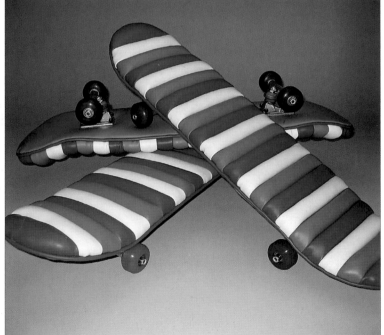

0882 DIDI DUNPHY, USA

0884 AI KIJIMA, USA

0885 AI KIJIMA, USA

0886 AI KIJIMA, USA

0887 AI KIJIMA, USA

0888 CARRIE REICHARDT AKA THE BARONESS, UK

0889 CARRIE REICHARDT AKA THE BARONESS, UK

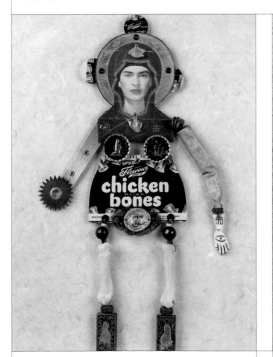

0890 LINDA AND OPIE O'BRIEN, USA

0891 LINDA AND OPIE O'BRIEN, USA

0892 LINDA AND OPIE O'BRIEN, USA

0893 MARY ENGEL, USA

0894 MARY ENGEL, USA

0895 MARY ENGEL, USA

0896 MARY ENGEL, USA

0897 JANE PIERCE, ZJAYNE, USA

0898 JANE PIERCE, ZJAYNE, USA

0899 DRÉK DAVIS, USA

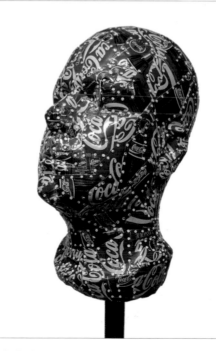

COURTESY OF FOLEY GALLERY, NY

0900 THOMAS ALLEN, USA

0901 ANGUS MARK BUNGAY, CANADA

0902 HELENA WEHRSTEIN, CANADA

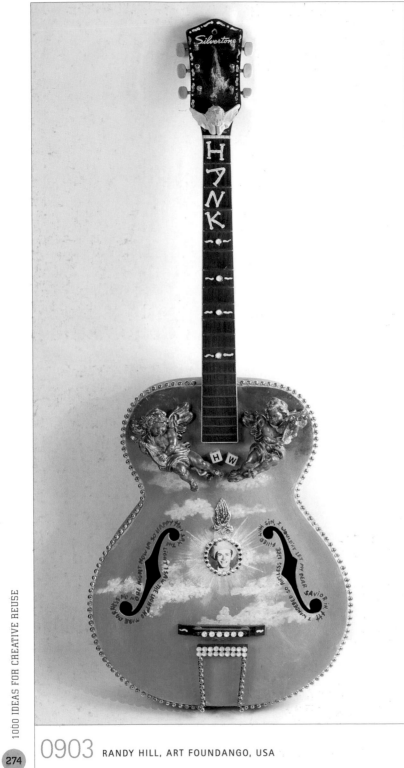

1000 IDEAS FOR CREATIVE REUSE

0903 RANDY HILL, ART FOUNDANGO, USA

0904 AMY RUBIN FLETT, USA

0905   MILAN MICICH,
TOKENS & ICONS, USA

PHOTO BY GEORGE POST PHOTOGRAPHY

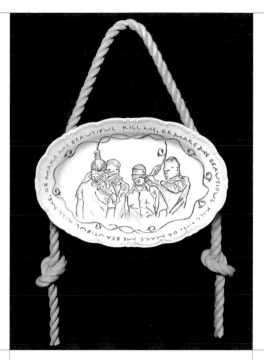

0906   HANS BOOY AND
PAULUS FUGERS, GERMANY

0907   AMY M. SANTOFERRARO, USA

0908   ELIZABETH LUNDBERG MORISETTE, USA

0909   KEN FLETT, CANADA

ART, INSTALLATIONS + INTERIORS

275

0910 TIFFANY THREADGOULD, REPLAYGROUND, USA

0911 JON BEINART, TODDLERPEDES, AUSTRALIA

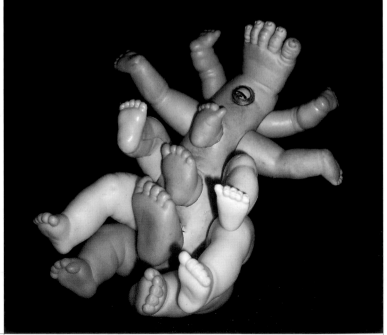

0912 JON BEINART, TODDLERPEDES, AUSTRALIA

0913 AMY RUBIN FLETT, CANADA

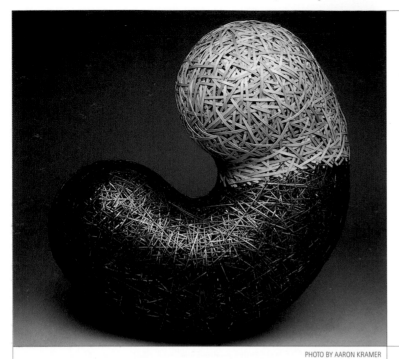

0914 AARON KRAMER, URBAN OBJECTS, USA

0915 AARON KRAMER, URBAN OBJECTS, USA

0916 HELEN NODDING, AUSTRALIA

0917 MARI KASURINEN, FINLAND

0918 SAYRAPHIM LOTHIAN, AUSTRALIA

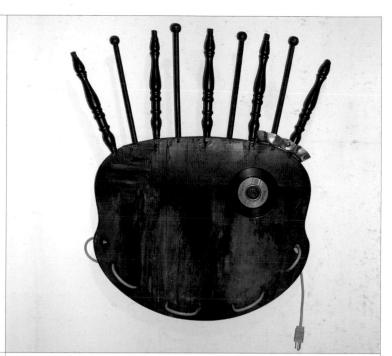

0919 DRÉK DAVIS, USA

PHOTO BY TOMMI MUSTANIEMI

0920 MARI KASURINEN, FINLAND

0921 DIDI DUNPHY, USA

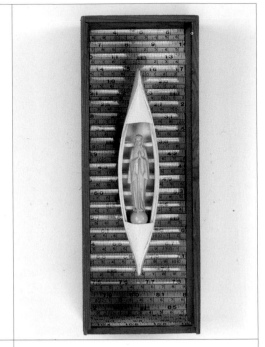

0922 HELEN NODDING, AUSTRALIA

0923 AARON KRAMER,
URBAN OBJECTS, USA

0924 VALERIE ARNTZEN, CANADA

0925 UNDINE BROD, USA

0926 ROMY SAI ZUNDE, INSECTUS ARTEFACTS, AUSTRALIA

0927 MAX LIBOIRON, USA

ART, INSTALLATIONS + INTERIORS

0928 DEREK VON ESSEN, CANADA

0929 LAURA PRENTICE, USA

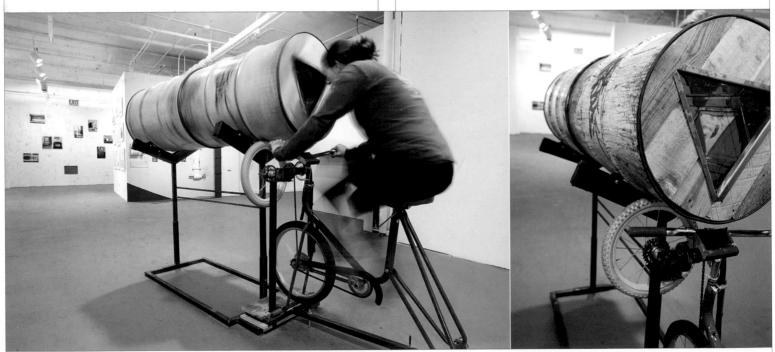

0930 HEATHER YOUGHDAHL MULLINS, USA

ALISON WILDER, USA

0932 ALISON WILDER, USA

0933 ALISON WILDER, USA

0934 ALISON WILDER, USA

ART, INSTALLATIONS + INTERIORS

283

0935 RANDY HILL,
ART FOUNDANGO, USA

0936 BEN SCHACHTER, USA

0937 BEN SCHACHTER, USA

0938 KIM BUCHHEIT, USA

0939 KIM BUCHHEIT, USA

0940 HANS BOOY AND
PAULUS FUGERS, GERMANY

0941 VIRGINIA GRISWOLD, USA

0942 VIRGINIA GRISWOLD, USA

0943 TERESA SULLIVAN, USA

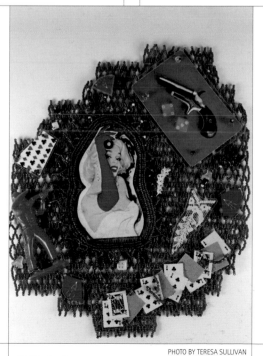

0944 TERESA SULLIVAN, USA

0945 TERESA SULLIVAN, USA

0946 SALLY CHINEA, UK

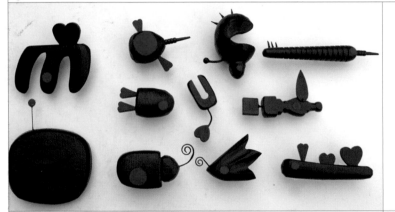

0947 HILARY PFEIFER, USA

0948 SARAH BALDWIN, USA

0949 BRIAN BENFER, USA

0950 CARRIE REICHARDT, AKA THE BARONESS, AND MR. SPUNKY, WITH HELP FROM THE TREATMENT ROOM, UK

1000 IDEAS FOR CREATIVE REUSE

0951 BLAND HOKE, USA

0952 HELENA WEHRSTEIN, CANADA

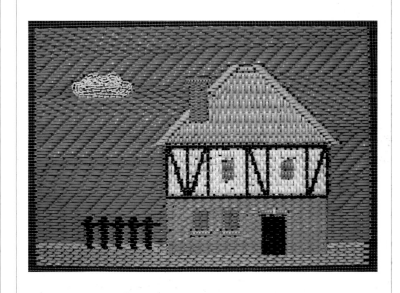

0953 BEN SCHACHTER, USA

0954 KEITH LINTON, USA

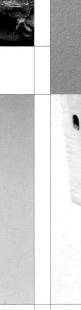

PHOTO BY STEVE BARALL

0955 VIRGINIA GRISWOLD, USA

0956 STANTON HUNTER, USA

0957 MEG J. ROBERTS, USA

0958 MEG J. ROBERTS, USA

0959 BLAND HOKE, USA

0960 PATRICK DOUGHERTY, USA

0962 PATRICK DOUGHERTY, USA

0961 PATRICK DOUGHERTY, USA

0963 PATRICK DOUGHERTY, USA

0964 RON MIRIELLO, MIRIELLO GRAFICO, INC., USA

0965 ALISON WILDER, USA

0966 STANTON HUNTER, USA

0967 PATTI HASKINS, USA

0968 RON MIRIELLO, MIRIELLO GRAFICO, INC., USA

0969 MERLIYN DEGRAAF, JULIA DE JONG, AND MIEKE FOKKINGA, THE NETHERLANDS

0970 PATTI HASKINS, USA

0971 PATTI HASKINS, USA

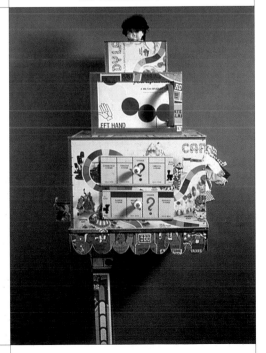

0972 LAUREL NATHANSON, USA

0973   AUDREY MOLINARE, ERIN BURKE,
AND DANIELLE BENSON, USA

0974   JEFF ALEXANDER, JALEX STUDIOS, USA

0975   SAYAKA SUZUKI, USA

0976   THOMAS P. JONES, USA

0977 JANELLE IGLESIAS, USA

0978 HONGTAO ZHOU, USA

0979 HONGTAO ZHOU, USA

0980 BLAND HOKE AND MATT RINK, USA

0981 BLAND HOKE AND MATT RINK, USA

0982 SAYAKA SUZUKI, USA

0983　GUERRA DE LA PAZ, USA

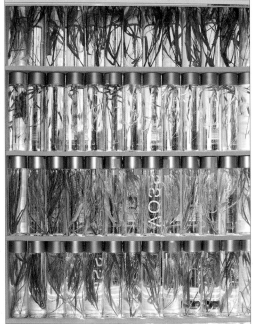

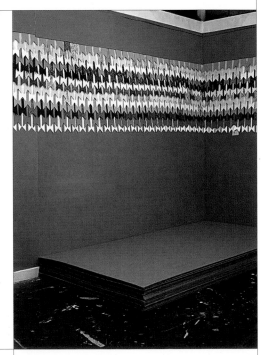

0984　HILARY PFEIFER, USA

0985　MICHELLE KAUFMANN, USA

0986　AUDREY MOLINARE, USA

0987 JAROD CHARZEWSKI, USA

0988 GUERRA DE LA PAZ, USA

0989 GUERRA DE LA PAZ, USA

0990 CARRIE REICHARDT AKA THE BARONESS
AND MR. SPUNKY, UK

0991 CARRIE REICHARDT AKA THE BARONESS
AND MR. SPUNKY, UK

0992 CARRIE REICHARDT AKA THE BARONESS
AND MR. SPUNKY, UK

0993 CARRIE REICHARDT AKA THE BARONESS
AND MR. SPUNKY, UK

0994 GUERRA DE LA PAZ, USA

0995 GUERRA DE LA PAZ, USA

0996 GUERRA DE LA PAZ, USA

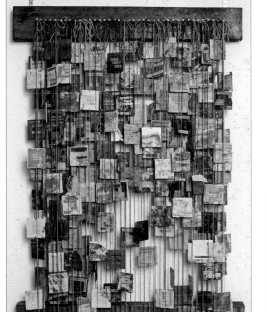

0997 SARAH BALDWIN, USA

ART, INSTALLATIONS + INTERIORS

0998 JANELLE IGLESIAS, USA

0999 ALLEGHANY MEADOWS, USA

1000 JANELLE IGLESIAS, USA

RESOURCES

Blogs and Websites

1000 Ideas for Creative Reuse www.creativereusebook.com
AfriGadget www.afrigadget.com
Craft Magazine Blog blog.craftzine.com/archive/green
Crafting a Green World www.craftingagreenworld.com
Craftstylish www.craftstylish.com
Design*Sponge www.designspongeonline.com
Dudecraft www.dudecraft.com
Extreme Craft www.extremecraft.com
GoUSAproducts gousaproducts.com
Haute Nature www.hautenature.blogspot.com
Instructables www.instructables.com
Re-Nest www.re-nest.com
Supernaturale.com www.supernaturale.com
Superuse www.superuse.org
Treehugger www.treehugger.com
West Coast Crafty www.westcoastcrafty.com

Organizations

Trillium Artisans www.trilliumartisans.org

Recycle Centers for Alternative Art Materials

Art from Scrap www.artfromscrap.org
Arts and Scraps www.artsandscraps.org
East Bay Depot for Creative Reuse
    www.ciwmb.ca.gov/reuse/Profiles/EastBay.htm
Hudson Valley Materials Exchange www.hvme.com
Materials for the Arts www.mfta.org
Materials Resource Center www.craftmaterialsresource.com
Recycled Materials Center www.kidmuzm.org
Recycle Shop www.bostonchildrensmuseum.org/exhibits/recycle.html
Resource Depot www.resourcedepot.net
The Scrap Box www.scrapbox.org
The Scrap Exchange www.scrapexchange.org
SCRAP—The School and Community Reuse Action Project
    www.scrapaction.org
SCRAP—Scroungers' Center for Reusable Art Parts www.scrap-sf.org
St. Louis Teachers' Recycle Center
    www.stlouisteachersrecycle.homestead.com
Urban Source www.urbansource.bc.ca

Videos and Publications

Make Magazine www.makezine.com
ReConstruct DVD www.reconstructdvd.com
Readymade Magazine www.readymade.com

IMAGE DIRECTORY

0001 Altered Books **0002** Peach Fade Vessel; recycled paper, wheat paste, acrylic paint, polyurethane **0003** Like a Glove Miniature Book; leather from old ladies' gloves, buckle from same ladies' gloves, Arches Text Wove paper, decorative flocked paper, binder's board, linen thread **0004** Untitled (Gold Paper Bowl); recycled paper, wheat paste, acrylic paint, polyurethane, gold leaf **0005** Yellow Fade Vessel; recycled paper, wheat paste, acrylic paint, polyurethane **0006** Reincarnation Too; found drawer, plaster figures, metal Buddha, industrial mixer, salvaged glass tiles, wood patterns, paper lanterns, acrylic paint **0007** Recycled Grocery Bag Cards **0008** Hot Little Numbers; Postconsumer recycled telephone book, paper, tea bag envelopes, cardboard coffee cup sleeves, egg crate, thread, ink **0009** Dairy Diaries; milk cartons, recycled paper, waxed linen thread **0010** Recycled Grocery Bag Card Set **0011** Vintage Book Wallets; salvaged fabric book covers and/or pages, salvaged sheets, pillowcases, and curtains, zipper, thread **0012** Recycled Magazine Pendant; magazine page, glue, jewelry findings **0013** Orange Bop Journal; various recycled papers, including recycled ledger book pages and "while you were out" message pages, chipboard cover, polypropylene film **0014** Game Plan; vintage game pieces, wood filler, papier-mâché boxes, ephemera **0015** Vintage Book Wallets; salvaged fabric book covers and/or pages, salvaged sheets, pillowcases, and curtains, zipper, thread **0016** Personal Journal; found books and paper, paint, glue, glitter, teeth, stones, binding varnish **0017** Vintage Book Wallets; salvaged fabric book covers and/or pages, salvaged sheets, pillowcases, and curtains, zipper, thread **0018** For Song Birds; collage **0019** Charcoal Envelope Stack; Laura Ashley wallpaper, PVA glue **0020** Thoughts To Go To Sleep With; journal pages, thread **0021** Recycled Paper Bead Necklace; paper, sterling silver **0022** Blue Star; collage, mixed media **0023** Encyclopedia Blocks; old encyclopedias **0024** Scrap Journal; book board, various recycled papers **0025** Garbage Mailart Alphabet Postcard; frozen food box backing with parts from discarded books, magazines, calendars, wrapping paper, photos, acrylic paint and acrylic gel **0026** "Pilgrim's Progress" Journal; vintage book, reclaimed pages including wallpaper samples, maps, and dictionary pages, ribbon, vintage button **0027** Red Dayplanner; recycled book covers, papers, linen thread **0028** Tribute; collage **0029** Bed (Open); collage **0030** Meanderings Journal; junk mail, paper sacks, dress patterns, wrapping paper, maps, waxed linen thread, acrylic paint, buttons, copper tape, chipboard coaster, beads, and washers **0031** Stinging Nettle; collage **0032** Aggravation Journal; cast-off papers from thrift stores, used books, and the artist's collection, waxed linen thread **0033** Garbage Mailart Alphabet Postcard; frozen food box backing with parts from discarded books, magazines, calendars, wrapping paper, photos, acrylic paint and acrylic gel **0034** For Bees; collage **0035** Fish Box; shadow box, found objects, ephemera **0036** Garbage Mailart Alphabet Postcard; frozen food box backing with parts from discarded books, magazines, calendars, wrapping paper, photos, acrylic paint and acrylic gel **0037** Recipe Mailer Cards; vintage imagery from old cookbooks, cardstock, kraft envelope, thread **0038** Tarot Card Notebook; tarot cards, scrap paper **0039** Sushi Grass Tapestry; magnet wire, plastic sushi grass, plastic sushi flower garnishes, old cotton rice bag, needlepoint netting and nylon mesh **0040** Old School Bookkeeping Book; recycled book covers, papers, linen thread **0041** Eco Journal with Hemp Tie; reclaimed paper, natural dyed hemp **0042** Woven Notebook; security envelopes, index cards, grommets, book rings **0043** Eco Reporter Journal; reclaimed paper, cotton thread, bookbinding tap **0044** Ultimate Sketchbook No. 1; self-healing cutting mat, recycled book cover, paper, linen thread **0045** Eco Journal; reclaimed paper, cotton thread, bookbinding tap **0046** Stack of Books; recycled book covers, papers, envelopes, linen thread, love **0047** Cardboard Loom Journals; cardboard mailer, scrap yarn, scrap fabric, scrap paper (pages) **0048** Recycled Address File Box; magazine subscription cards, vintage and found paper, unfinished wooden box, wood stain, varnish, cardstock, rub-on letters **0049** Resurrection; printer box, stainless-steel grid, glass tiles, copper, vintage crucifix, beeswax **0050** Detail Page from "Threads"; vintage photo album page, vintage photo, ephemera, origami paper, thread **0051** Handmade Book **0052** Detail cards from "Box of Cards"; backs from old tablets, ephemera, acrylic paint **0053** Plaid Party Dress #1; vintage cookbook covers, nails, paper, on wood **0054** Fairy Tale Tote ("Pony waits to give Baby a ride"); salvaged curtain, salvaged sheet, page from the children's book *Baby's Pets*, vintage leather button **0055** Philip Simmons; bottlecaps **0056** The Center of a Red Clay Trail; reclaimed 1968 army sergeant's uniform, dog tags, broken toys, reclaimed Vietnam War postcard, aerogram and '60s Vietnamese postage stamp, revisited 1970s antiwar song lyrics, thrift store bible, text using vintage typewriter **0057** Leigh; bottlecaps **0058** Recycled Magazine Vase; magazine pages, wine box, glue **0059** My Secret Identity; pages from damaged comic books, glue and pen on paper **0060** My Secret Identity; pages from damaged comic books, glue and pen on paper **0061** My Secret Identity; pages from damaged comic books, glue and pen on paper **0062** Detail cards from "Box of Cards"; backs from old tablets, ephemera, acrylic paint **0063** Recipe Mailer Cards; vintage imagery from old cookbooks, cardstock, kraft envelope, thread **0064** Random Images + Thoughts Notebooks; vintage imagery from old books, chipboard, 100% postconsumer Enviro100 paper, staples, thread **0065** Dreaming of Spring Gardens; recycled paper and envelope, image is created with recycled seed catalogs **0066** Notecard for Knitters; recycled paper and envelope, image is created with recycled knitting and yarn catalogs **0067** Eco Note Box; reclaimed chipboard, reclaimed paper, Mod Podge, hot glue **0068** Drop It (greeting card) **0069** School of Fish; coin envelopes, recycled paper, book board, ribbon **0070** Tarot Fan; authentic tarot cards (paper) **0071** Marble 8-Ball; reclaimed marbles and bowling ball **0072** Excerpt of Studies: Assignments, Sketches, and Notes; old school papers **0072** Excerpt of Studies: Assignments, Sketches, and Notes (detail); old school papers **0073** Paint Chip Notebooks; paint chips, scrap paper, linen thread **0074** The 1955 Book; record, thrift store girdle, damaged leather, crayon wax, repurposed plastic, discarded wood, book excerpts, newspaper clipping, found photographs, handmade paper from 1950s women's magazine, metal,

and 1950s song lyrics **0075** French Calendar Purse; Garbage Art French Calendar Purse **0076** Number Journal; cast-off papers from thrift stores, used books, and the artist's collection, double wire-o binding, buttons, waxed linen thread **0077** Personal Journal; found books and paper, paint, glue, glitter, teeth, stones, binding varnish **0078** Eagle Fall; collage **0079** Man's Stationery Box (Altered Cigar Box); cigar box, bingo card, charms, collage images, stickers, ephemera **0080** I Hear a Symphony; musical instrument parts, Christmas lightbulb, sheet music, box (manufacturer's second), picture frame **0081** We Go Together; musical instrument parts, sheet music, box (manufacturer's second), picture frame **0082** When I'm Sixty-four; musical instrument parts, sheet music, box (manufacturer's second), picture frame **0083** Bosun; old fabric, wood, leather, thread, silver print on old tent canvas, beeswax **0084** Fortune Tapestry **0085** Bottlecap Mosaic Fish; assorted bottlecaps, plywood, recycled car body metal, rake **0086** Modern Ruins 4; used papers, pencil, paint, stitching **0087** La Siren; bottle caps, vitreous glass, carved wood, enamel paint, copper, glass eyes **0088** Modern Ruins 2; used papers, pencil, paint, stitching **0089** Racket (greeting card) **0090** The Matronly Ghost; Kleenex, cat saliva **0091** Note Cards; old children's school books, adhesive tabs, note cards **0092** Recycled Paper Earrings; paper, sterling silver **0093** Modern Ruins 1; used papers, pencil, paint, stitching **0094** Modern Ruins 3; used papers, pencil, paint, stitching **0095** Plaid Party Dress #2; vintage cookbook covers, nails, paper, on wood **0096** Harlen on Ice; peanut shell, pipe cleaner, acorn top, pom-pom, old metal zipper, felt, paper clips, skirt hooks, rickrack, fabric, metallic cord, bead, nail polish, glue, thread, google eyes **0097** Personal Journal; found books and paper, paint, glue, glitter, teeth, stones, binding varnish **0098** Garbage Mailart Alphabet Postcard; frozen food box backing with parts from discarded books, magazines, calendars, wrapping paper, photos, acrylic paint and acrylic gel **0099** Stock Samples Notebook; various old and unused paper samples and paper samples packaging **0100** Random Images + Thoughts Mini Cards; vintage imagery from old books, cardstock,

manila envelope, thread **0101** Personal Journal; found books and paper, paint, glue, glitter, teeth, stones, binding varnish **0102** Smashing; corduroy, sheer, silk, satin **0103** Storm; cotton **0104** Puppetress; corduroy, silk **0105** Octopus Buttondown; recycled denim, buttons, machine-stitched appliqué on vintage men's shirt **0106** Broken Record; sheer, silk **0107** Backgammon Set; board made from 2X men's shirts, game pieces made from recycled paper pulp and acrylic paint **0108** Garbage Bag Bag; black and white garbage bags, orange flagger's tape, trash-rescued linen place mat, recycled zipper and shoulder strap **0109** Casey; recycled fleece vests, neckties, buttons, polyfill **0110** Basic Upcycled Card Holder; used vinyl banner, thread, cardboard **0111** Recycled Sweater Handbag **0112** Dollar Sign Pillows; vintage fabric **0113** The Black Stallion Book Purse; vintage hardback children's book, 100% cotton quilting fabric, wooden beads on metal frame, vintage button and grosgrain ribbon **0114** Old Suit, New Purse; vintage suit coat for body, vintage bed linens **0115** Corazon Tejido (apron); handwoven fabric made from plastic bags, caution tape, yarn, corn husks, plastic strawberries, loteria card, belt, wire, tarp, nylon webbing **0116** T-Scarves; recycled T-shirts **0117** Ethella, Mythical Katamari Cousin; upcycled cotton clothing **0118** Dress; recycled prom dresses, vintage lace **0119** Prairie Dress; thrifted flannel sheets **0120** Flower Brooch; old sheet, buttons **0121** Twila; hand-painted and -printed recycled fabric and clothing, commercial fabrics, vegetable bag plastic net, raffia, paint, thread, beads **0122** Earl Nil; hand-painted and -printed recycled fabric and clothing, commercial fabrics, vegetable bag plastic net, raffia, paint, thread, beads **0123** Vestiges of Fall; hand-painted and -printed recycled fabric, recycled clothing, commercial fabrics, vegetable bag plastic net, raffia, thread **0124** Maple; hand-painted and -printed recycled fabrics, spray painted table linens, shabori dyed recycled sheets, commercial fabrics, vegetable bag plastic net, thread **0125** Catsugars **0126** Owls Family; reused textile felt, wool filling **0127** Green Alien; recycled gloves and mittens **0128** Little Green Mitten Man; recycled gloves and mittens **0129** Little Purple Mitten Man; recycled gloves and mittens **0130** Striped Monster Hat; felted sweater wool, T-shirt pieces, felt, vintage buttons, thread **0131** Turkey Pattern Dress; repurposed Thanksgiving stuffed turkey pattern fabric **0132** Chinatown Red Plastic Bag iPod case; exterior: plastic bags, plastic mesh, recycled paper **0133** Madras Bow Tie; vintage necktie, thread, adjustable slider **0134** Cashmere Scarflet; cashmere from recycled sweater, embellished with lambswool from recycled sweater, secondhand buttons, and thread **0135** Sail Luggage Tag; Dacron sailboat sails, organic cotton canvas, sail, insignia cloth, nylon webbing, rayon trim **0136** Paper Scarf; recycled paper, silk thread **0137** Sandstone Colorblock Sweater; recycled merino wool, lambswool, wool, and vintage buttons **0138** Sail B Purse; Dacron sailboat sails, organic cotton canvas, sail, insignia cloth, nylon webbing, rayon trim **0139** Unicorn Bow Tie; vintage necktie, thread, adjustable slider **0140** Pumpkin Pie **0141** Almost Naked Rabbit Skirt; recycled vintage cotton, polyester and voile fabrics, buttons, machine embroidery, machine-stitched appliqué on rayon skirt **0142** Lamenting Owl Jacket; cotton, recycled vintage silk and polyester fabrics, tulle, machine-stitched appliqué on vintage wool jacket **0143** Mustache Deer Skirt; cotton, recycled denim, vintage polyester, vintage buttons, machine-stitched appliqué on rayon skirt **0144** Scout Finch Skirt; recycled vintage cotton and polyester fabrics, buttons, hand and machine embroidery, machine stitched appliqué on vintage cotton skirt **0145** Smoking Shark Jumper; vintage cotton and polyester fabrics, buttons, machine-stitched appliqué on vintage cotton dress **0146** Shrug; zippers and thread **0147** Pucker; zippers and thread **0148** Striped Scarf and Cuffs; reconstructed sweaters **0149** Ramona (apron); handwoven fabric made from plastic bags, yarn, sponges, flash card, typewritten letter, vinyl tablecloth, rubber gloves, ribbon **0150** Watermelon Bag; reused place mat, vinyl, kayak strap **0151** Bird Tote; reused jeans, reused belt, ribbon, felt **0152** Yellow Flowers Reversible Mini Messenger Bag; recycled vintage pillowcase and recycled denim jeans **0153** Roz's Messenger Bag; recycled plastic bags, plastic fence mesh **0154** Alexander Handbag; recycled suit coats **0155** Chase Handbag; recycled suit coats **0156** Chase Handbag; recycled suit coats **0157** Suit Coat Scarf; recycled suit coats **0158** Suit Coat Scarf; recycled suit coats **0159** Sidney Handbag; recycled suit coats **0160** Measuring Up Purse; metal eyelets, wire,

metal snap **0161** White Plastic Bag Party Dress; white cotton underdress with white plastic bags overdress. Grocery bag strung on string **0162** Cardboard Shell Gown; cardboard boxes lined with cotton and connected with packing string **0163** Black Trash Bag Couture Gown; black plastic trash bag panels knotted into a gown with a train **0164** Remade Vintage Slippers; Asian newspaper, tulle and scrap fabric **0165** Aluminum Gown; natural cotton corseted underdress with aluminum overlay and silver buttons **0166** Brown Paper Bag Gown; natural cotton underdress hand-dyed brown with organically torn brown paper attached **0167** Recycled Sail 35 Tote; Dacron sailboat sails, organic cotton canvas, sail, insignia cloth, nylon webbing, rayon trim **0168** Cirque de Doll; silk, lace, cotton **0169** Brand Identity Jacket; clothing care, size and brand labels, gold satin, interfacing, thread **0170** Roadster Clutch; recycled inner tubes, recycled red scrap fabric and thrifted red zipper **0171** Egyptian Necklace #1; denim, embroidery thread, organic cotton batting, shell button and thread **0172** Bike Tire Wallet **0173** Sail Messenger Bag; Dacron sailboat sails, organic cotton canvas, sail, insignia cloth, nylon webbing, rayon trim **0174** gLOVE Bag; vintage zipper and fabric from old dress, vintage button, vintage bracelet, vintage glove **0175** Rezoom Bunny Bag; inner tubes, fur, steel cable, plastic tube **0176** Rezoom Duster; inner tubes, rivets, studs **0177** Sweet Meats Deli Wrap; butcher paper **0178** Sweet Meats - Little Ham; 100% recycled fleece, fiberfill and dyes with new felt and plastic button embellishments **0179** Sweet Meats - Little Pork; 100% recycled fleece, fiberfill and dyes with new felt and plastic button embellishments **0180** Boiled Egg and Toast Soldiers; recycled felt, polyfill, embroidery thread **0181** Liquorice Allsorts; recycled felt, polyfill, embroidery thread **0182** Sweatshirt Sushi Mitts; sweatshirt, T-shirt pieces, sock pieces, thread, chopsticks **0183** Black Bubbles Bitty Bean Silk; recycled fabric sample, Interior: 100% silk, new zipper **0184** Ginko Leaf Tapestry **0185** Bucket Hat; used tea towel **0186** Lingo Game Board Packing Tape Purse; Dumpster rescued game board and lining, grocery bag rope handle **0187** Kitten Child Skirt; tea towel, tablecloth, recycled fabric, elastic **0188** Poppies Child Skirt; vintage decorative pillow, knit fabric, corduroy, elastic **0189** Kirin Light Sunglass Clutch; beer boxes **0190** Winter Calendar Slippers; tea towel, batting, cotton, vinyl **0191** Oilcloth Wallets;

oilcloth, reclaimed marine vinyl, thread, zipper, western snap, ink **0192** Black Dog YEAH; reused textile felt, wool filling **0193** "Clown Pants" Handspun Art Yarn; reclaimed wool, cast-off yarn & thread scraps **0194** Pac-Man Dress; repurposed children's bedsheet **0195** 2008 Emmy Invitation (front); eco-friendly cotton garment bag, YDG silk-screened water-based inks **0195** 2008 Emmy Invitation (back); eco-friendly cotton garment bag, YDG silk-screened water-based inks **0196** Bingson; recycled fleece vests, neckties, buttons, polyfill **0197** Shirt Dress **0198** Skirt Dress **0199** Sweater Pants **0200** Sweater Pants **0201** Assorted Recycled Sweater Balls; recycled sweaters of various fiber content, thread, polyester fiberfill **0202** Circus Childs Dress; vintage shower curtain, vintage fabric **0203** Compai's Table Top; vintage crocheted tablecloth, hemp bias binding **0204** Love Medicine; felted wool and cashmere from discarded garments **0205** Stilted Modesty; run pantyhose, wire **0206** Bubble Necklace Group; recycled T-shirts, batting, thread, snaps **0207** Willow Sweatervest; recycled lambswool, wool, and vintage buttons **0208** Patchwork Tea Wallet; linen fabric, patchwork made with recycled tea packaging, vintage button, vintage ribbon, thread **0209** Medusa; repurposed XXXL vinyl snakeskin pants **0210** Telescopic Bubble; cotton, polyester, lace **0211** Dress; vintage slips and lace, hand-dyed **0212** Two Tone Blue Denim Reversible Purse; recycled vintage duvet cover and recycled denim jeans **0213** Faux Faux Bois; upcycled cotton clothing **0214** White Dove Sweatervest; recycled lambswool and vintage buttons **0215** "Stash Tea Bag" Pocketbook; empty tea bag wrappers, thread **0216** Knitted Neck Sausage Links Scarf; 100% recycled lambswool/wool/angora/nylon yarn **0217** Blue Jean Comfort; blue jean scraps, Harley-Davidson patch **0218** Asymmetrical Blue Tweed Wallet **0219** Gangrene Vintage 50s Sweater—Patient No. 4; seafoam acrylic yarn and green/white unknown yarn, over 36 operations performed **0220** Recycled Jeans and Shirt Hat **0221** City Boy goes Country!; recycled men's shirts **0222** Glitter Fun Little Bean Silk; recycled fabric sample, Interior: 100% silk, new zipper **0223** Recycled Sweater Cozies; old wool sweaters, embroidery floss **0224** Cherry Blast Little Bean; recycled oilcloth fabric sample, Interior: recycled fabric sample, new zipper **0225** Bird Blanket; cotton shirt, linen blouse, vintage terry, fabric scraps, bias, batting **0226** The Lord of the Rings Paperback

Wallet Collection; paperback book, waterproof vinyl, fabric edging tape, elastic, vinyl pockets **0227** Algebra Book Purse; vintage hardback textbook, 100% cotton quilting fabric, wooden beads on metal frame, vintage button and grosgrain ribbon **0228** Vesty of the Basins Book Purse; vintage decorative hardback book, Liberty of London cotton fabric, acrylic beads with metal spacers on a metal frame, vintage button and grosgrain ribbon **0229** Plane Geometry Book Purse; vintage hardback textbook, 100% cotton quilting fabric, wooden beads on metal frame, vintage button and grosgrain ribbon **0230** The Joy of Cooking Book Purse; vintage hardback cook book, 100% cotton quilting fabric, wooden beads on metal frame, vintage button and grosgrain ribbon **0231** Cassette Tape Coin Purse; cassette tape, coin purse clasp, fleece **0232** Farmer's Market Recycled Onion Bag Totes; 50 lb. onion bags and oilcloth **0233** Bike Tire Belts; bike tires, belt buckles, belt bolts, thread **0233** Bike Tire Belts (detail); bike tires, belt buckles, belt bolts, thread **0234** Vintage Cardigan—Patient No. 19 **0235** Kid's Hoodie; upcycled cashmere sweaters **0236** Heather Grey Baby and Kids' Slippers; recycled sweaters and recycled leather **0237** ReWrap It; men's wool pants, preserving pocket details **0238** Marching to the Beat of the Cats Jacket; cat hair from Doggie and Mitzie, boiled wool fabric, snaps and thread **0239** Homage to Doctor Zoidberg; upcycled cotton clothing **0240** Carotenemia—Patient No. 24 **0241** T-Scarf; recycled T-shirts **0242** Recycled Sweater Cozies; old wool sweaters, embroidery floss **0243** T-Shirt/Box Purse; cardboard box, T-shirt **0244** Shoulder Bag; used bedspread cover and button **0245** Harley Quilt; old Harley-Davidson T-shirts, Harley-Davidson patches **0246** Fortune Cookies; thrifted sweaters **0247** "Grape Ape2" Handspun Art Yarn; reclaimed wool, cast-off yarn and thread scraps **0248** "Madras Madness" Handspun Art Yarn; recycled sari silk thrums, vintage mohair yarn **0249** Denim Cuff; recycled jeans and T-shirt, with top-stitched thread embellishment **0250** PBR CD Case; beer case, vinyl, CD sleeves, elastic, and thread **0251** The Regan, Blue; two recycled long-sleeved, button-down, cotton, collared shirts **0252** Eco-Friendly Kids Art Smock; 100% cotton women's blouse embellished with 100% cotton fabric **0253** Victoria's Secret Box Purse; Victoria's Secret gift boxes **0254** Basic Upcycled Clutch Purse; used vinyl banner, thread, Velcro **0255** Basic Upcycled Clutch

Purse; used vinyl banner, thread, Velcro **0256** Stripe Tee; upcycled T-shirts **0257** Recycled Skateboard Belt Buckle; broken skateboard decks **0258** Basic Upcycled Long Purse/Wallet; used vinyl banner, thread, cardboard **0259** Disc-O Bag; old floppy disks and broken electrical wire **0260** Recycled Rainbow Sweater Ball; recycled sweaters of various fiber content, thread, polyester fiberfill **0261** "Green Man" Handspun Art Yarn; reclaimed wool, silk and cotton fabric remnants **0262** Circe's Camisole; recycled plastic bags, danger tape, tape, Velcro closures **0263** Circe's Tote; recycled plastic bags, plastic fence mesh **0264** Pot Holder Patty Top; vintage pot holder, recycled/reclaimed fabrics, thread, ribbon **0265** Jade Mixmaster Top; recycled cotton jersey T-shirts **0266** Rezoom Blue Sweater Dress; recycled sweaters **0267** Rezoom Brown Sweater Dress; recycled sweaters **0268** Ascension **0269** Split Decision **0270** Fair Isle Baby and Kids' Slippers; recycled sweaters and recycled leather **0271** Necktie Hairbands **0272** Medium Plarn Basket; crocheted postconsumer plastic (HDPE) grocery sacks **0273** Recycled Leotard Dance Bag **0274** Paper Scarf; recycled paper, silk thread **0275** Phoenix Sweater; reconstructed and recycled lambswool, wool, and vintage buttons **0276** teddycookie **0277** A-Line Skirt; used tablecloth and a doily **0278** Broken Image 1 Apron; reclaimed fabrics including reassembled lined tea towel **0279** Horizon Dual Panel Apron; recycled fabrics including men's work shirts and pants **0280** Red Mongol Skirt; recycled fabrics including woolen pants, men's neckties, and tablecloth **0281** Waratah Skirt; recycled fabrics including fragmented Waratah-print linen tea towel **0282** Yellow Blanket Skirt; wool blanket, vintage sheet, bias **0283** Caution (apron); handwoven fabric made from caution tape, yarn, rubber inner tube, nylon webbing, leather, ribbon **0284** Shooting Hoops (apron); basketballs, leather jacket, handbag strap, kid's notebook, netting **0285** Measuring Up Wallet; metal eyelets, wire, metal snap **0286** Chicken Feed Messenger Bag; reused plastic woven chicken feed bag, recycled shirt material **0287** Sinews in the Swamp Dress; gym T-shirt, recycled t-shirts, curtain drapes, found buttons, recycled lace, thread **0288** Cobalt Blue and Pure White Vintage Fabric Belt; recycled vintage fabric, webbing, D-rings **0289** Bag O' Gold Little Bean Silk; recycled fabric sample, Interior: 100% silk, new zipper **0290** The Treehugger Headhugger; repurposed scarf, sweater and a sock without a mate

0291 Melanocytosis Vintage 50s Sweater—Patient No. 5; blue acrylic yarn, 1 operation on the front, 1 on the right side, and 1 on the back **0292** Green Dress; used sheet **0293** Sweet Meats—Little T; 100% recycled fleece, fiberfill and dyes with new felt and plastic button embellishments **0294** Recycled Plastic Bags Zipper Pouch; plastic bags from newspaper delivery fused together to make fabric, zipper **0295** Purple Berries Messenger Bag; recycled corduroy trouser lined with recycled vintage bed linen **0296** Bank Logo Pillows; vintage fabric **0297** Kid's Hat; felted sweater **0298** Vintage Moygashel Dilly Tote Bag; recycled vintage curtains **0299** Obama Campaign Poster Purse; cardboard campaign poster, cloth hinge **0300** Paper Scarf; recycled paper, silk thread **0301** Recycled Sweater Coozies; old wool sweaters, embroidery floss **0302** Mittens; upcycled cashmere sweaters **0303** Postbag; reused Dutch PTT canvas postbag **0304** APR Pillows; vintage fabric **0305** Lux's Tux; old work shirt **0306** No Pain Stain; wine-stained shirt, embroidery floss **0307** Asymmetrical Herringbone Tweed Wallet; thrifted and salvaged men's suits **0308** 'Mocha-mix Flower' Baby and Kids' Slipper; recycled sweaters and recycled leather **0309** 'Coffee and Cream' Baby and Kids' Slippers; recycled sweaters and recycled leather **0310** Large Plarn Basket; crocheted postconsumer plastic (HDPE) grocery sacks **0311** Asymmetrical Herringbone Tweed Wallet **0312** Eye Multi-Compartment Wallet; recycled billboard vinyl, metal snap **0313** Upcycled Earthy Hobo Bag; upcycled unraveled sweater **0314** Cashmere Dresses; upcycled cashmere sweaters **0315** Sunflower Barrette; reused sweater (cuff), yarn, embroidery floss, felt, button, barrette, glitter glue, hot glue **0316** Cento Pin; recycled Cento anchovy tin, recycled copper sheeting, recycled leaf/flower pin, copper plated frame, silver plated embellishments, brass rivets **0317** Charge!—Part of the Found Object Series; sterling silver, plastic toy **0318** Yellow Pages Girasole Earrings; recycled paper, glass **0319** Mary Lamb Comb; vinyl record, comb **0320** The Abacus Ring; tin can, newspaper, and glue **0321** Purple-K: A Postapocalyptic Cocktail Ring; corroded electrical conduit, silver, pale amethyst reclaimed from scrapped antique brooch, dark blue topaz, garnet **0322** Upcycled Phone Charm; origami stars made from Japanese television listings, black shell beads, surgical steel chain and black nylon cord **0323** Recycled Plate

Belt Buckle; recycled Johnson Brothers china, belt buckle **0324** Runway Necklace; reused rubber o-rings, recycled sterling silver, cubic zirconium, synthetic garnets, coated copper wire **0325** Now That's What I Call a Pearl Necklace; vintage playing cards, pearl necklace **0326** Time Capsule; brass, clockwork, peacock chain, found metal, found earring **0327** Tribal Elegance Collection: Silver Web; reused rubber, recycled sterling silver, coated copper wire **0328** District of Columbia Leather; DC token, distressed leather cord, aged pendant **0329** Colorado Springs Chain; Colorado Springs token, distressed ball-chain, aged pendant, hemp cord **0330** Winged Typewriter Key Necklace; sterling silver, WWII-era brass military wings, vintage typewriter key **0331** New York Subway Token Cuff Links; authentic 1950s-era subway token, sterling silver **0332** Indianapolis Leather; Indianapolis token, distressed leather cord, aged pendant **0333** Super Star Cuff Links; recycled bottle caps, sterling silver **0334** Worker Badge II; watchband, leather, Soviet-era pin **0335** Girasole Ring; recycled paper, glass **0336** White Cells: A Postapocalyptic Cocktail Ring; corroded electrical conduit, silver, large, pale citrine reclaimed from damaged antique cocktail ring, green cubic zirconium, garnets **0337** Victorian Sunset Airship, a Steampunk Fantasy; vintage, antique and estate jewelry, watches, crystals, watch parts, rhinestones, beads **0338** Pink Sheller Bracelet; recycled paper, copper **0339** Button Necklace; vintage buttons, vintage reclaimed beads, wire, string **0340** Postage Stamp Ring; vintage Norwegian postage stamp, sterling silver, resin **0341** Mixed Washer Bracelet; ½" (1.3 cm) steel washer, nuts and lock washers **0342** Zipper Spiral Pendant (Magenta); recycled vintage zipper, thread, glue, sterling silver jump ring **0343** hEarring Blossoms; sterling silver, plastic doll parts, resin **0344** The Kiss Necklace; sterling silver, plastic doll parts, resin **0345** Busted Heart Pendant; sterling silver, plastic doll parts, resin **0346** Starburst Hand Brooch; sterling silver, plastic doll parts, resin **0347** Profile Smile Brooch; sterling silver, plastic doll parts, resin **0348** Smiley Necklace on Torque; sterling silver, plastic doll parts, resin **0349** Don't Tell Fred; glass beads, printed tin toy, thread, glass bead necklace found at an estate sale along with a note card reading: "Lenore, Inside are beads from tassel. Maybe you can fix it. This is that one of Aunt Bess you liked..." **0350** Vintage Czech Postal Stamp Necklace **0351** Zipper Necklace with Blown

Glass Capsule Charm **0352** Postage Stamp Resin Necklace; vintage American postage stamp, sterling silver, resin, steel cord **0353** Button Bracelet; vintage buttons, vintage reclaimed beads, wire, string **0354** Round Envelope Pendants; security envelopes, pewter pendants, sealer glue, resin **0355** Vintage New Zealand Postal Stamp Necklace **0356** Frames; recycled aluminum cans, sterling silver **0357** Sea Glass Bracelet **0358** Sandy's Bracelet; hand-inked dominoes strung with beads **0359** Pearl Vintage Collage Bracelet; vintage pearl memory wire bangle, vintage pearl circle pin, vintage cluster clip earring, E-6 adhesive **0360** Last Supper Plate Ring; recycled Last Supper plate, silver-plated ring blank **0361** Omphalos; linoleum and vinyl samples, button **0362** Victorian Waltz, a Steampunk Fantasy; vintage, antique and estate jewelry, watches, crystals, watch parts, rhinestones, beads **0363** Love Tree Fork Necklace; steak fork bent to hold vibrant Swarovski crystals and pearls, vintage glass beads, clear glass beads **0364** Matchbox Cuff; matchbox, matches, wire, and wood glue **0365** Tally Silver Ring; recycled paper, sterling silver **0366** Dog License Cuffs **0367** Chandelier Light Necklace; chandelier lights, vintage collected cameos, leather **0368** Bullet Bracelet Bullet; brass bullet cartridges (recycled), garnets **0369** Hearts and Flowers Necklace; silver American coins, sanded and reformed; sterling silver **0370** The Newspaper Cuff; newspaper, metal buttons **0371** Everyday Regalia Necklace **0372** Anellini in a Silver Coat; precious metal clay, sterling silver, citrine beads, homemade pasta **0373** Watch Face Necklace; collected watch faces, jewelry findings **0374** Nutty Necklace; steel nuts, lock nut, and crystal cabochon **0375** Gear Earrings; steel machine gear, silver tone bead, decorative bead **0376** Tribal Necklace; sanded and reformed silver American coins, sterling silver **0377** Sunflowers and Daisies Bracelet; sanded and reformed silver American coins, sterling silver **0378** Concept Rings; steel retaining rings, sterling silver rivet **0379** Forgotten Necklace; sterling silver, freshwater pearls, vintage watch case, tintype photograph **0380** Bog Oak with Concrete Inlay; ancient bog wood, concrete **0381** Rosewood Ring Set with Birch Inset; salvaged rosewood from a guitar, birch **0382** Bog Oak Band with Saharan Sand; ancient bog wood that has been preserved in the peat bogs of Europe for 5,000 years, sand from the Sahara Desert **0383** Pearl Spotted Bangle; audiocassette

tape, acrylic yarn, found object, freshwater pearls **0384** Letterpress Pendant **0385** Feather Concept Rings; sterling silver, feathers, polymer clay **0386** Teak with Pearl Wood Ring Set; salvaged teak wood, crushed pearl from old jewelry and buttons **0387** Nature's Barcode #2; FSC Certified Brazilian Garapa, salvaged exterior decking and shipping pallet material, sourced from waste bin compost pile **0388** Periwinkle Dream; swag chain from ceiling lamp, organza ribbon from gift wrapping, copper wire, goldstone beads, 13 mm spring clasp, jump rings **0389** Vintage Girl; watch, typewriter keys **0390** Reclaimed Teak Bangle; reclaimed teak flooring planks from a demolished shipping container **0391** 3 Piece Band, Stacking Ring Set; reclaimed walnut, salvaged white oak and yellow heart **0392** Rubber Band Bracelet; rubber bands **0393** Moretti Aspen Leaf Beerings; Moretti LaRossa beer bottle glass, copper foil, copper rod, lead-free solder **0394** Knotty Olive Wood Cuff; olive wood salvaged from cabinet makers' trash bin **0395** Roadsigns; recycled aluminum cans (color disk), sterling silver **0396** Zipper Daisy; recycled zippers and buttons **0397** Stitch/type (necklace); computer keys (recycled), nylon, sterling silver, stainless steel **0398** Bedroom Eyes; vintage sheet music and vintage mattress **0399** Upcycled Gift Card Ring **0400** Lone Star Beer Ring; upcycled steel, Formica **0401** Baseball Stitches Cuff Links **0402** Sushi Earrings; tin can, drinking straws, and resin **0403** Conditions Apply (earrings); computer keys (recycled), nylon, sterling silver **0404** Star Pendant; bottlecap, broken jewelry bits, recycled magazine paper, resin, findings **0405** Recycled Skateboard Necklace; broken skateboard decks **0406** Pins and Needles; aluminum knitting needles, sterling silver **0407** Nana 100% (brooches); vinyl Nana Mouskouri records (recycled), brass, milk bottle tops, pen parts **0408** Vintage Button Rings **0409** Azian Garden Spoon Bracelet; silver spoon etched with an Asian-influence foliage design **0410** Recycled Zipper Bracelet; recycled zippers, spray paint, jump rings, wire, crimp beads, glue, clasp **0411** Uranium Yellow: A Postapocalyptic Cocktail Ring; corroded iron electrical conduit, silver, large lemon citrine, blue topaz, peridot, tourmalines **0412** Green Ring; old ring, thread, embroidery floss, beads **0413** Postage Stamp Teardrop Earrings; vintage postage stamps, sterling silver, seed beads, cardstock paper, laminate **0414** Scrabble Tile Pendants; thrifted paper, thrifted Scrabble tiles, gel medium, spray lacquer, sterling silver finding **0415** Fresh Clean Scent (40 Loads series); sterling silver, plastic laundry detergent cap, epoxy resin, Prismacolor, patina **0416** Doll Eyelash Earrings; vintage plastic doll/monster eyelashes from the '70s and vintage glass Mardi Gras beads **0417** Bottlecap Collage Pendant; bottlecap, broken jewelry bits, recycled book paper, resin, findings **0418** Pen Power Pins (tie pins); brass bullet cartridges (recycled), pen nibs **0419** Maize-n-blue; linoleum sample **0420** SAL Collection: SAL Ring; recycled produce rubber bands, sterling silver **0421** Oval Champagne Bracelets; recycled tin cans, brass, plastic core **0422** British Invasion; found items **0423** Flatliners (pins); plastic toys (policemen and firemen), brass **0424** SAL Collection: SAL Ring; recycled produce rubber bands, sterling silver **0425** Zipper Necklaces with Blown Glass Capsule Charms; hand-altered zippers, hand-blown borosilicate glass, cut-up copper wire, miniature fork, a cruelty-free feather, metal findings **0426** Plastic Animal Leg Ring; recycled plastic animal legs and oxidized sterling silver **0427** Disc Chic Necklace; polymer clay (premo), aluminum disks taken apart from computer stuff, findings, Millefiori canes, chain **0428** The Newspaper Rings; newspaper, adjustable ring base **0429** START . FOCUS . recycled negatives earrings; recycled film negatives, hypoallergenic hooks **0430** The Newspaper Cuffs; newspaper, metal buttons **0431** Coke Chatter; embossed Coca-Cola disks on ball chain **0432** Recycled Skateboard Rings; broken skateboard decks **0433** Recycled Plate Necklace; recycled Johnson Brothers china, sterling silver, lead-free solder **0434** Motherboard Cuff Links **0435** The Raven (necklace); framers scrap acrylic, cutout from Victorian animal book 1885, copper **0436** Repurposed Vinyl Bracelet; water jet-cut vintage record **0437** Soft Spike Bracelet; reused rubber parts, recycled sterling silver **0438** Button Choker; thrifted buttons, jewelry wire and findings **0439** Upcycled Vinyl Record Earrings **0440** Zipper Necklace; secondhand metal jacket zippers, sewing thread **0441** Bike Tire Bracelet **0442** Basic Black Classic—a Roman Record Cuff; recycled vinyl record **0443** Zipper Daisy; recycled zippers and buttons **0444** Guitar and Bass Strings Bracelets **0445** Tin-Tastic: The Whole 9 Yards; metal, recycled tin cans, game pieces, found materials, resistors, pop tops, rivets **0446** Trash to Treasure Bracelet; tin, computer boards, dried-out paint tubes, old tobacco

metal and metal game boards **0447** Time After Time; watch, typewriter keys **0448** Worker Badge I; watchband, leather, Soviet-era pin **0449** Feeling Naughty; 16-gauge closed S-hooks, copper wire **0450** Azian Imagination Fork Bracelet; etched and transformed serving fork **0451** My Sweet Memories; recycled metal rimmed key tags with family photographs **0452** Island of Googlies; precious metal clay, sterling silver, boulder opal cabochon, carnelian cabochons, carnelian beads and handmade recycled paper **0453** Girl Inside a Bottlecap; bottlecap, broken jewelry bits, paper, resin, findings **0454** Trio Mura Ring; paper **0455** There's a Bird on My Gate Post; pendant, vintage chain, rhinestones, sawed-off metal gate post, metal pieces, glass beads **0456** Williams Sonoma Bracelet; recycled tin cans, brass, Plexiglas, plastic core **0457** Push the Button Brooch; tin can, paper, and resin **0458** Circles ReCycle Cuff; clean plastic shopping bags cut into yarn **0459** Orange Ring; old ring, thread, embroidery floss, beads **0460** Happy Retro Rocket; upcycled steel, formica, German silver **0461** Recycled Skateboard Earrings; broken skateboard decks **0462** Flower ReCycle Cuff; clean plastic shopping bags cut into yarn **0463** Medieval Lady; watch parts, scrap metal, vintage chain, playing card section, metal pieces from old jewelry, plastic button, rhinestone **0464** Hidden Under Coral; audiocassette tape, acrylic yarn, bamboo coral, found object, onyx, shell **0465** Roger and Blithe; street sign, sterling silver, copper, ball chain **0466** Stars and Sparke Earrings; steel lock washers and steel fender washer **0467** New York Road Trip Bracelet **0468** City Bird; street sign, license plate, sterling silver, copper, various chain, vintage bead, fiber **0469** Unlock Bangle Spoon Bracelet; vintage spoon, vintage key, sterling silver **0470** Unlock Bangle Butter Knife Bracelet; vintage butter knife, vintage key and sterling silver **0471** Hearsay Heart; street sign, sterling silver, copper, ball chain **0472** Zipper Necklaces; hand-altered titanium and blue zipper, handblown borosilicate glass capsule charm **0473** Rectangles; linoleum samples **0474** Upcycled Credit Card Ring **0475** Discarded Bible Pages Beads; pages from a discarded Bible, polyacrylic sealer, glass accent beads **0476** Resistor Necklace; old TV and radio resistors and capacitors paired with salvaged thrift store chains **0477** Madamoiselle; brass, clockwork, found metal, repurposed chain, glass **0478** Vintage Bourbon Liquor Necklace **0479** The Murindi Necklace; recycled native

Australian wood **0480** Recycled Security Envelopes Paper Beads; security envelopes turned inside out and rolled into beads, polyacrylic sealer, seed beads and Swarovski crystals **0481** Upcycled Hotel Room Key Bracelet **0482** Lemon Drops on My Tongue; precious metal clay, sterling silver, citrine beads, handmade recycled paper **0483** Bouncing Pearls on a Snare Drum; precious metal clay, sterling silver, cultured pearls, handmade recycled paper **0484** Vintage Watch Parts Necklace; vintage watch faces, parts and gears, jewelers epoxy, glass and pearl beads, base metal chain and findings **0485** Take Your Time; watch, typewriter keys **0486** Vicodin Earrings; generic Vicodin tablets, silver-plated jewelry findings **0487** Square Antique Button Ring; fine silver bezel, sterling silver sheet, half round sterling silver wire, antique metal button **0488** Loose Change Jewelry; real coins **0489** Steampunk Bat; section of old drawer pull, earring parts, found copper charm, beads, old chain **0490** Assemblage; linoleum and vinyl samples **0491** Matonella; recycled paper, glass **0492** Purple Record Cuff; recycled vinyl record, acrylic paint **0493** Feng; glass beads, thread, doll arm, buttons, decorative poker chip **0494** Button Bracelet **0495** Guitar String Hoops; 26 gauge 'D' guitar string, sterling wire, sterling silver earwire **0496** Cake Earrings; Japanese teen magazine, plastic rhinestones from a child's sticker, Swarovski crystal findings, surgical steel earwires **0497** Totem Series; repurposed vintage chains, vintage metal button, druzy quartz, recycled copper firebrick, dry creek jasper, recycled sterling silver **0498** Guitar String Drops; unwound guitar strings, wound bass string, sterling ear posts, sterling silver wire **0499** Wooden Button Necklace; upcycled wooden button, paper, silver chain **0500** Timepiece Conversion; empty watch face, beading cord, sterling silver toggle clasp, amber nugget beads, sterling silver bali-style rondelle beads, Swarovski crystals, oval amber cabochon **0501** Blue Ring; old ring, thread, embroidery floss **0502** Doily Earrings; sterling silver wire, hand-colored paper doilies, resin **0503** Recycled Plate Necklace with Stained Glass; recycled Johnson Brothers china, lead-free solder, sterling silver, stained glass **0504** Spent Bullet Necklaces; old bullet casings paired with vintage glass beads and salvaged thrift store chains **0505** Vintage Button Charm Bracelet **0506** Trash Bling Rings; sterling silver, broken jewelers saw blades, eggshells, *New York*

Times newspaper delivery bag, epoxy resin **0507** Needle-Link Necklace; aluminum knitting needles, sterling silver **0508** Britto Bracelet; recycled tin cans, brass, plastic core **0509** Rotorcaps; recycled bottle caps, nickel silver, stainless steel **0510** 7 Strand Junk Mail Beads; real junky junk mail, polyacrylic sealer, seed beads **0511** Jangly Earrings; aluminum knitting needles, sterling silver **0512** Button Barrettes; vintage buttons, metal barrette clasps, glue **0513** Recycled Keyboard Pin; bottlecap, circuit board of a keyboard, paper, resin, finding **0514** Button Earrings; vintage buttons, vintage reclaimed beads, wire, string **0515** Argent Bubbles in Crimson; precious metal clay, sterling silver, enamel, cherry quartz beads, lava stone beads and handmade recycled paper **0516** Vacuum Tube Necklace; old vacuum tube **0517** Monkey Shine; molded plastic, wool, rubber from inner tube **0518** Sunday Comic Paper Beads; Sunday comic paper from the Sunday newspaper, polyacrylic sealer and accent "cat's eye" beads **0519** Gold Vintage Collage Bracelet; vintage gold-tone brooch, vintage resin brooch, vintage gold bangle, E-6 adhesive **0520** Bike Tire Bracelet **0521** Blue Sunset on the Grey Lagoon; corroded, welded iron from a lobster pot, silver, discarded sewing machine needles, discarded dental burr, discarded galvanized steel, porcelain "faux coral," freshwater pearls, aventurine, aquamarine, peridot, amethyst, ne **0522** Stone. Cold. Fox! **0523** Maintenent; WWII-era vintage Swiss watch, brass, sterling wire, sand, cutting from a vintage book, pearls **0524** T.W.E.R.P.; 10" (25 cm) Mad*L (vinyl), Bleep Labs Thingamakit, Lexan, spray paint **0525** Cart Bike; bicycle and shopping cart **0526** Rolling Rock Drinking Glasses; Rolling Rock Bottles **0527** CD Sleeve; disk protective sleeve from outdated electronics **0528** The Scrabble Keyboard; Scrabble tiles, brushed aluminum casing, oak faceplate **0529** Oblong (with circuitry); resin, recycled computer circuit, bail, bezel **0530** Spotty (on computer piece); resin, recycled computer circuit, bail, bezel **0531** Pointer (side); resin, recycled computer circuit, bail, bezel **0532** BC2 and Triangulate; resin, recycled computer circuit, bail, bezel **0533** Digi; resin, recycled computer circuit, bail, bezel **0534** Circuit Ray; resin, recycled computer circuit, bail, bezel **0535** Man-orah; repurposed plumbing pipe **0536** Brass and Marble LCD Mod **0537** Striped Ceramic Insulator Necklace; oxidized sterling silver and recycled ceramic insulators **0538** Malt Machine; old stove legs, dentist's drill, sewing

machine parts **0539** TV Table; wood, old baseball cards, glue, acrylic gloss, resin **0540** Red Stripe Drinking Glasses; Red Stripe bottles **0541** Barron Cyclops; espresso machine parts, bicycle gears, vintage flour sifter, coffee pot bottom, car door handles, C.B. antenna base springs, towel rack mounts **0542** Flamegirl; rusty tin **0543** Manhole Concert Poster (Wolf Eyes); silk-screened LP **0544** Reel Clock; 1" (2.5 cm) video tape reel, clock kit **0545** Eject Earrings—Part of the Computer Jewelry Series; sterling silver, fine silver, plastic computer key **0546** Key Invader; keyboard keys, plastic sheet **0547** Escape—Part of the Computer Jewelry Series; sterling silver, fine silver, plastic computer key, aquamarine stone **0548** Manhole Concert Poster (Growing); silk-screened LP **0549** Ceramic Insulator and Fishing Lure Brooch; oxidized sterling silver and recycled ceramic insulator and fishing lure **0550** Manhole Concert Poster (Rizzudo); silk-screened LP **0551** Eject—Part of the Computer Jewelry Series; sterling silver, fine silver, plastic computer key **0552** Steampunk Sewing Machine; vintage sewing machine, brass and copper findings, wool yarn **0553** Scrap Flowers; tin vase, electronic connectors and wire **0554** "Lander People" stool; old golf clubs and wooden shelf **0555** Triple Modular Candlestick; scrap electronic connectors (polished aluminum) **0556** Tiny Toys in Resin (Like Carbonite); plastic toy, resin **0557** Tiny Toys in Resin (Like Carbonite); plastic toy, resin **0558** High Chair; wooden ladder, 1960s pod chair, builders pine **0559** Westinghouse; found objects **0560** GID AsteroiDunny: RED MARS; 8" (20 cm) Dunny, polymer clay, spray paint, acrylic paint **0561** Elgin; found objects **0562** EIMAC; vintage Eimac vacuum tube, freewheel bicycle gears, copper pot, car door handles, corkscrews, industrial machine parts **0563** Menakis Tree; found items, lighting and wiring **0564** Robo Rescue; old desk bell, light socket, sink hose, electrical conduit elbows, water valve handles, child's coinsafe, fire alarm pull switch, motorcycle foot pegs, vintage chalk line **0565** G5 Lamp; Apple G5 water-cooled dual processors, LED lights, aircraft compass, hour-meter, misc. hardware **0566** Mario Mechno; found Items **0567** Plasma Dunny; 8" (20 cm) Dunny, plasma globe, wood, stainless steel, rubber, acrylic paint **0568** Driftwood Bike **0569** T-34 Blaster; candlestick, hacksaw, motorcycle hand brake, lamp parts, plumbing valve ball, tool box handle **0570** The Opti-Transcripticon; modified flatbed scanner **0570** The Opti-Transcripticon (detail);

modified flatbed scanner **0571** Flight/Racing Simulator; van passenger seat, scrapped industrial Vacuum motors, junk computer monitor, scrap metal, PVC pipe, computer steering wheel controller and scavenged keyboard **0572** Modular Candlestick; (BNC) connectors, copper **0573** Speaker; speakers, fiberglass mannequin, 1/8 stereo jack, power/volume knob, hand-built solid-state stereo amplifier **0574** Guitar Hero Tin Figure; rusty tin, leather **0575** Amplifier; car speaker, Ikea lamp, hand built amplifier **0576** Ski Bike **0577** Great Bowl O' Fire; 500 gallon propane tank, inner rim of forklift wheel, car spring **0578** Ammo Box Synth; 7.62 mm caliber ammo box, modified synthesizer kit **0579** MP3 Grenade; Sansa 1GB Mp3 player embedded in a surplus decommissioned training grenade **0580** FirePit; repurposed stainless-steel washing machine drum **0581** Dancing Devil Recycled Steel Firebowl; 150-pound propane tank **0582** Scooter Bike; old two-by-four with crank bearings set in a hole, Razor Scooter front end and plywood wheel stays, misc. bike parts and coaster brake back wheel **0583** Electronics Earrings; capacitors, potentiometers, silver-plated jewelry findings **0584** Arctic Steampunk Raygun; candlestick, pewter mug, bicycle gear, lamp parts, springs, nuts, bolts, brass drawer pull, mixer handle, wood burning stove handle **0585** Monite Man; license plate lamp, Monite glue tin, bicycle brake, washing machine gears, spring base mounts from C.B. antenna, bicycle clamp levers **0586** GEORGIA Hat; cardboard boxes, T-shirt, game program picture, cloth liner **0587** Titleist Golf Ball Box Hat; golf ball boxes, cloth liner **0588** Mirrors; wood, old baseball cards, glue, acrylic gloss, resin **0589** Tray; wood, old baseball cards, glue, acrylic gloss, resin **0590** NASCAR Hat; beer boxes, old NASCAR calendar, cloth liner **0591** Scorecard Hat; scorecards, cloth liner **0592** Gummy Candy Hard Hat; gummy candy, superglue **0593** 21st Century Breastplate; reused circuit boards, reused rubber, brass **0594** Hedorah Custom; Bandai Hedorah, spray paint, acrylic paint **0595** Electronics Earrings; capacitors, potentiometers, silver-plated jewelry findings **0596** Tiny Toys in Resin (like Carbonite); plastic toy, resin **0597** Ceramic Insulator Ring; oxidized sterling silver, recycled ceramic insulator, vintage glass ball **0598** Volcon; found objects **0599** Ceramic Insulator Bracelet; oxidized sterling silver, recycled ceramic insulators **0600** Runway Circuit; reused circuit boards, gold colored copper wire

0601 Twinings; found objects **0602** Erase 2—Part of the Computer Jewelry Series; sterling silver, fine silver, plastic computer key, aquamarine stone **0603** Eco-Friendly Pocket Protector; repurposed vintage suit coat and new iron-on vinyl **0604** 78 Label Concert Poster (Fonotone); silk-screened LP **0605** iPod Speaker Madness; chemistry plumbing glass, extruded aluminum, vintage train headlight glass, Mac Pro speakers, amplifier, garden trowels, garden forks, thermos canister lids, various unidentified vintage glass items **0606** Photo Studio; translucent storage box, desk lamps, construction paper **0607** Plastic Bottle Car; plastic bottles, electric motor, rubber ring, wire, battery **0608** Annie Ceeze; keyboard keys, female torso (plastic) **0609** Datamancer's Steampunk Laptop; HP laptop computer, wood, copper and brass **0609** Datamancer's Steampunk Laptop (detail); HP laptop computer, wood, copper and brass **0610** IBM Model M Ergo Keyboard; curved brass keyboard with acanthus-leaf etching **0611** Wine Barrel Armchair; American Oak Barrique, PVA, Timber glue **0612** EcoBirdfeeder; wooden chopsticks and wood glue **0613** Annie; repurposed shopping cart **0614** Side Kick Table; white oak and galvanized steel bands from wine barrels, smoky burgundy highlights **0615** Maison Royale (table); reused 3" x 8" (7.5 x 20 cm) spruce floor joists and beams **0616** Max; repurposed vintage cast-iron bath **0617** Simple Green Recycled Bike Clock; recycled bicycle chain ring, reclaimed textile, quartz clock movement and metal clock hands **0618** 6-Pack Vase; aluminum cans, plastic **0619** Plasma Planter; metal tube (former scientific equipment), rocks, soil, succulents of various sorts, caulk, 2 metal screens **0620** Pilsner Urquell Oak Leaf; Pilsner Urquell beer bottle glass, copper foil, copper rod, lead free solder **0621** Volivik lamp family: Bic pens lamp collection; Volivik 50 table lamp, White structure, cristal green biros **0622** Pinky; porcelain and glass **0623** Moss Rug; mill ends ripped into strips of fabric—linen, rayon, cotton **0624** Repurposed Upholstery 2; screen-printing textile pigment on found salesman samples **0625** Hötorgslampa/Scrapped Art Lamp; discarded paintings, discarded lamp structures **0626** Tiny Bakelite Frame 4; Bakelite, vintage plastic, postcard **0627** Anatomy of a Murder; recycled wood, books, whisk **0628** Mail Box Reused as Sideboard **0629** Tangerine Recycled Bike Clock; recycled bicycle chain ring, reclaimed textile, quartz clock movement and metal clock hands **0630** Reading Chair; recycled wood, books, pencils **0631** Inversion; recycled wood, books **0632** Unboxed Lamp; aluminum rods, newspaper, extension cords **0633** Triple Bulge Chandelier; recycled tin cans **0634** Our Flesh and Blood; reclaimed Persian and Afghani scrap wood from broken furniture, wood scraps, FSC plywood, and piece of truss **0635** Tub Chair; repurposed utility sink seat, reclaimed carpet underlay cushion, scrap plywood rocking sled base **0636** Trophy Coat Rack; trophies, wood, paint, metal picture frame, nails, guitar string **0637** Atomic Eggbeater Clock; eggbeaters, wood, paint, clock movement **0638** Tan Recycled Corduroy Log Cabin Pillow; recycled corduroy pants, vintage and stash patterned fabric, thread **0639** Vintage Feedbag Pillow **0640** Antique Bottle Dryer Light Fixture **0641** Eco-Friendly Soy Candles in Reused Wine Bottles; organic soy wax, wine bottles **0642** Tiny Bakelite Frame 6; Bakelite, vintage plastic, postcard **0643** Philadelphia Upperware; slip-cast porcelain, decals, found caddy **0644** 5 Fancy Lanterns; recycled tin cans **0645** Skull and Crossbones Place Mat; discarded burlap wholesale coffee bean sack, broken bicycle inner tube, polyester thread **0646** Beer and Wine Bottle Bottoms Mobile; beer bottle bottoms, copper rods and swivels **0647** Oregon Tea Towel Café Curtains; tea towels, curtain rings **0648** EcoBirdfeeder; wooden chopsticks and wood glue **0649** Goth Clock; recycled vinyl record, acrylic paint, clock movement and hands **0650** Brown Recycled Corduroy Log Cabin Pillow; recycled corduroy pants, vintage and stash patterned fabric, thread **0651** Box/Table Packaging Concept; cardboard **0652** Stepped Record Bowl; vinyl record **0653** Reb Web Weave (chair); reclaimed corrugated cardboard **0654** Rockabilly Record bowl; recycled vinyl record, acrylic paint, semigloss polyurethane **0655** Lamplanta: plant growing floor lamp **0656** Pilar—Floor Lamp **0657** Ted's CRANKshaft Lamp **0658** PAPERKNIFE SCISSOR; black plated steel **0659** Upcycled Clock; thrifted plastic clock & wallpaper **0660** Vases to Go; recycled bottles, glass paint **0661** Upcycled Alarm Clock; thrifted alarm clock & wallpaper **0662** Dressed Up Office Chair; IKEA Agen children's wicker chairs, slip covered in cotton fabrics **0663** Artificial Sweetener Tablecloth; artificial sweetener packets, packing tape **0664** Chinese Checkers Night Table; game board, table, paint, glass **0665** Child's Bureau; bureau, leftover paint, sea glass, assorted colored glass **0666** Pot Rack Table; salvaged cabinet door, stair spindles, scrap wood and pot rack **0667** Side Table; salvaged marine grade plywood, concrete **0668** Spacetime; car taillights, scrap diamond plate, pot lids, clock, lights **0669** Toothpaste Vase and Flowers; toothpaste tube, trophy base, nut, adhesive, detergent bottle, swizzle sticks, wire **0670** Tiny Bakelite Frame 5; bakelite, vintage plastic, postcard **0671** Vase; discarded wool sweater **0672** Tobacco Tin Pincushion; antique store find Prince Albert Cigarette Tobacco tin, reused sample upholstery fabric swatch **0673** Eco-Friendly Soy Candles in Reused Wine Bottles; organic soy wax, wine bottles **0674** Sullivan headboard **0675** Jellyfish Chandelier; recycled tin cans **0676** KOZO2; galvanized iron parts, electronics, ceramic parts, iron tap **0677** Emma in Coffee Stirrer Basket; reclaimed coffee stirrers and metal strapping **0678** Omaka Bord/ Uneven Table; broken furniture pieces, paint **0679** Exploding Briefcase, Chandelier; salvaged aluminum briefcase, aluminum rod, electrical parts **0680** Wine Glass Markers; assorted tokens, distressed ball-chain, hemp cord **0681** BE WHERE? D.P.W. Platter®; recycled aluminum traffic signs, copper rivets **0682** Ticket Bowl; paper ticket roll, Mod Podge **0683** Sweeper Bristle Basket **0684** Ballbasket; plastic baseball charms and cotton **0685** Rustic Songbird Bowl; gourd, wood burning, paint, clear coat **0686** Vintage Feedbag Pillow **0687** Phone Book Pen Organizer; recycled phone book **0688** 45rpm Clock; vinyl record, acrylic stand, clock motor, aluminum hands **0689** Tiny Bakelite Frame 2; Bakelite, vintage plastic, postcard **0690** Work Table; salvaged marine-grade plywood **0691** Kurrency Chandelier; dollar bills, bent wire, plastic core with standard chandelier bulbs **0692** Orange MicroFilm Basket; woven microfilm **0693** Coke Float Sundae Glasses; Coca-Cola bottles **0694** Book Vase-round; test tube, repurposed book **0695** Spoon Mirror; reclaimed silver spoons, mirror, and beads **0696** Curvature Modern Lamp; 2 vases, napkin ring holder, window rod finial **0697** The Doors Collections: Introspective and Coherence; recycled door, place settings **0698** Headboard from Railing **0699** NYC Transit Chairs, "Times Square/42nd Street" marker **0700** D.O.T. Coasters® (assorted); recycled aluminum traffic signs **0701** Taxi Medallion Clock; authentic 1990s taxi medallion, authentic New York yellow taxi metal used as base, clockworks **0702** PENTATRAYS®; recycled aluminum traffic signs **0703** Yarn Spun Lampshade; vintage wire frame lampshade, yarn **0704** Mixer Light; mixer, ceiling light fixture **0705** Jet Set Lounge Chair; skateboard decks with cushions, metal frame **0706** Invisible Green; glass bottles **0707** Deluxe Spiral Chandelier; recycled tin cans **0708** Boats, 2002–2009; recycled hardwood bowls **0709** Vintage Feedbag Pillow **0710** Dawn hanging lamp; scrap plastic miniblinds, metal, pendant light fixture **0711** Spice Shakers; etched glass shakers **0712** Natural Rorschach; reclaimed burlwood from thrifted furniture, FSC Certified lumber **0713** ReMake It wine cork trivet; steel, wine corks **0714** Book Vase 1; test tube, repurposed book **0714** Book Vase Close-up **0715** Reading Lamp and Heavy Read Table; repurposed books, reclaimed metal and wood **0716** Reading Lamp and Heavy Read Table; repurposed books, reclaimed metal and wood **0717** Electrolux Lamp; 1937 Electrolux Vacuum, an old/found ceiling lamp, a lightbulb from the local thrift shop **0718** Aluminum Bird; recycled soda cans **0719** Aluminum Ball Ornament; recycled soda cans **0720** Altoids Advent Calendar; MDF, candy tins, spray paint, adhesive, number decals **0721** Hardware Snowflake Ornaments; assorted hardware, wire, ball chain **0722** Old Atlas Ornaments; recycled vintage atlas, copper wire **0723** Necktie Pillow **0724** Button Wreath **0725** Green Mustache Mug; etched coffee mug **0726** Three Transit Chairs, "MIR," "DETO," and "WEIGHT LIMIT"; reused aluminum traffic signs, champagne corks, steel hardware **0727** Hawaiian Record Bowl; recycled vinyl record, acrylic paint, semigloss polyurethane **0728** Lighthouse Window; old window, assorted colored glass, smalti glass, pebbles, Spanish moss, seashells **0729** HER D.P.W. Platter®; recycled aluminum traffic signs, copper rivets **0730** By Emmaus Collection **0731** Repurposed Vinyl Record Clocks; vintage records, custom clock movement **0732** Granny Square Rug; crocheted recycled T-shirts **0733** Octopus Pint Glass; etched pint glass **0734** Killer Bee, Mechanical Chandelier; salvaged dental drill, sunglass lenses, electrical parts, printer motors, window screen, miscellaneous hardware, brass, aluminum **0735** I've Always Wanted That Guy's Mustache; slides, old lamp-shade frame **0736** Mustache Pint Glass; etched pint glass **0737** Volivik Lamp Family: Bic pens lamp collection; Volivik 347 ceiling lamp, black structure, orange and black pens **0738** Exotica Modern Lamp; mango wood vase, candle holders **0739** Robot

Pint Glass; etched pint glass **0740** ReMake It bottle lamp; steel, recycled bottles, lighting fixture **0741** Metal Ducts=Lights (Organic Variation); metal ducts salvaged from renovation **0742** Metal Ducts=Lights (Sylo); metal ducts salvaged from renovation **0743** Stay Tab Lampshade; stay tabs from aluminum cans **0744** Modern Diamond Recycled Bike Clock; recycled bicycle chain ring, reclaimed textile, quartz clock movement and metal clock hands **0745** Red Line Design Recycled Bike Clock; recycled bicycle chain ring, reclaimed textile, quartz clock movement and metal clock hands **0746** KOZO3; galvanized iron parts, electronics, ceramic parts, iron tap **0747** Bike Chain Bowl; repurposed bicycle chain **0748** Ode to Albers in Grey Plastic; plastic bags, vinyl inner tube, styrofoam cord, plastic ribbon on monk's cloth **0749** KOZO1; galvanized iron parts, electronics, ceramic parts, iron tap **0750** Cassette Tape Chandelier; cassette tapes, wire, and chain **0751** Buckle Up Key Holder; reused seatbelt buckle and recycled aluminum **0752** Wine Barrel Folding Chair; white oak from salvaged wine barrels, smoky burgundy highlights **0753** Stax Chair; skateboard decks, bent plywood **0754** Barrel Head Toilet Seat; white oak from salvaged wine barrels **0755** Crackle; remelted window glass **0756** Sittlumpar/ Sit Rags; discarded textiles, new black textile, packing belt **0757** Street Spam Lounger; corrugated plastic signs **0758** Oh Deer Plate and Mug Set; vintage plate and mug, black enamel paint **0759** Udda Röd/Odd Red; found porcelain, ceramic decals **0760** Steel Sprout; bent stainless-steel tube sections **0761** Receipt Rug: I Own This; sales receipts, electronics packaging, tissue paper on monk's cloth **0762** Tsotchke Bowl; thrifted non-food-safe Japanese wooden bowl, scrap decorative paper from another project, a thrifted owl knickknack or tsotchke, gel medium **0763** 6-Pack Basket; heated 6-pack rings **0764** The Jenga Lamp; Bruce wood flooring, recycled window brackets, brushed metal cabinet legs **0765** Skanteria: shelf and coat hanger; reused skateboard **0766** Cathedral Time; table legs, scrap wood, flattened cans, metal conduit, metal pipe, clocks, thermometer, pool balls **0767** Cardboard Ottoman; corrugated cardboard, wood glue, biodegradable latex foam, fabric, duct tape **0768** Laptop Bag; discarded wool sweater **0769** Ice Bank; tempered window glass **0770** Receipt Rug: Pink (Is Still for Girls); sales receipts, plastic bags, feminine hygiene product wrappers, tissue paper on

nonslip rug pad **0771** Brown Mustache Mug; etched coffee mug **0772** Sail Pillow; Dacron sailboat sails, denim, sail insignia cloth, zipper, fiber fill insert **0773** Rezoom Happy Red Rocker; reclaimed chair, found objects **0774** Unboxed Chair and Ottoman; cardboard **0774** Unboxed Chair and Ottoman; cardboard **0775** Melting Plate; found porcelain plate **0776** Study in Blue; denim jeans, cotton backing **0777** Blue Grid; plastic bags, tissue paper, sales receipts on monkscloth **0778** Vases to Go; recycled bottles, glass paint **0779** Volivik lamp family: Bic pen lamp collection; Volivik 50 table lamp, White structure, cristal blue biros **0780** Melting Plate; found porcelain plate **0781** Melting Plate; found porcelain plate **0782** Rounded Couch with Table; half of an IKEA Sultan Sandane bed, pine board, corner brackets, screws, wood stain **0783** Vintage Feedbag Pillow **0784** Memories; 1959 Volkswagen engine cover **0785** God Father Lounge Chair; skateboard decks with cushions, metal frame **0786** Kurrency Chandelier; dollar bills, bent wire, plastic core with standard chandelier bulbs **0787** Layered Zipper Jar; recycled vintage zippers, glue, glass jar, metal lid **0788** Venn Moern Recycled Bike Clock; recycled bicycle chain ring, reclaimed textile, quartz clock movement and metal clock hands **0789** Recycled Lotto magnets **0790** Cheerful Frog Mason Jar Terrarium; Mason jar, pebbles, dirt, moss, plants, vintage frog figurine **0791** Bottle Green Mason Jar Terrarium; Mason jar, pebbles, dirt, moss, plants **0792** Caribbean Blue Recycled Bike Clock; recycled bicycle chain ring, reclaimed textile, quartz clock movement and metal clock hands **0793** Waffle Iron Jewelry Box; waffle iron, cake pan, wood, fabric **0794** Plarn Desk Caddy; clean plastic shopping bags cut into yarn **0795** Green MicroFilm Basket; woven microfilm **0796** Seena's Mirror **0797** Cork Mud Mat; wine corks, yoga mat (for the backing), glue **0798** Temper, Temper; tempered window glass **0799** Jesus Slept; old wall hanging **0800** Hang Up; polyurethane wheels and bearings, metal wires **0801** Green Flower; glass bottles **0802** Panty Coaster; old decorative panties, batting, bias **0803** Glass Weave; melted office window glass **0804** Glass Drinking Vessels; recycled bottles **0805** Recycled Rock and Roll 9 Album Jacket Coasters and Wood Caddy; album jacket, birch plywood, felt pads, glue, lacquer **0806** Pin Board; vintage shirt, thrift store frame **0807** Wrapped Wool Pincushion for Handsewing; recycled wool, thread, felt

0808 Astro Clock; polyurethane wheels and bearings, clock works **0809** Deer! D.P.W. Platter®; recycled aluminum traffic signs, copper rivets **0810** PANTIES drawer pulls; refrigerator magnets, sterling silver **0811** Trash Pillows; upcycled T-shirts **0812** Key Finder Wine Glass Charms; 1945, 1954, 1956, and 1958 West Virginia "key finders" **0813** 45rpm Ornaments; vinyl records, 45rpm adapter, bead chain **0814** Gallon Milk Jug Light Sculpture **0815** Safe from Harm; safe-deposit box, glass, casters **0816** Rosette Rug; crocheted recycled T-shirts **0817** Cinder Block Drawers; porcelain and glass **0818** L-Modern Coffee Table; Brazilian walnut parquet flooring, L-shaped wall shelving, recycled door, metal shelving brackets **0819** Melted Absolut Bottle Cheese Plate; melted vodka bottle **0820** Repurposed Upholstery 1; screen-printing textile pigment on found salesman samples **0821** Bin Seats—Mikla; repurposed garbage bin **0822** Repurposed Upholstery 3; screen-printing textile pigment on found salesman samples **0823** Crutch Stool; crutches, bicycle wheels, foam insulation, and bicycle inner tubes **0824** Reupholstered and Painted Silhouette Chair; acrylic paint, fabric, old wood chair **0825** Repurposed Upholstery 4; screen-printing textile pigment on found salesman samples **0826** Bin Seats— Office; repurposed garbage bin **0827** Chiquita Chandelier **0828** Bin Seats—Zevel; repurposed garbage bin **0829** Filing Cabinet Dresser; metal filing cabinets, nuts and bolts, hinges, casters, primer and homemade chalkboard paint **0830** Recycled Fabric Crochet Room Rug; fabric scraps, thread **0831** RED; repurposed vintage book **0832** MIGHT; repurposed vintage book **0833** TALE; repurposed vintage book **0834** SWELL; repurposed vintage book **0835** TANGLED; repurposed vintage books **0836** Carolina Wren; recycled credit cards **0837** Cardinal; recycled credit cards **0838** Hummingbird; recycled credit cards **0839** Goldfinch; recycled credit cards **0840** Early Bird; recycled coffee cans **0841** T-Bird; recycled tea tins **0842** Green Fiesta Jellyfish Lamp; postconsumer recyclable plastic containers **0843** BirdBrain; postconsumer recyclable plastic containers **0844** Freddy; postconsumer recyclable plastic containers **0845** Shimmering Red Runner; postconsumer recyclable plastic containers **0846** Royal Clockhead; postconsumer recyclable plastic containers **0847** Snub-Nosed Green Feeder; postconsumer recyclable plastic containers **0848** Swans **0849** Snowscape **0850** Roses **0851** Venus of Urbino **0852** Towel **0853** Dreams; plaster field jacket of an extinct Stylemys tortoise, plaster, ceramic **0854** Speed Demon; tach/dwell meter, glass beads, thread **0855** Border Town Girl #2; laminated paperback novel cover, glass beads, thread, natural-material beads **0856** Blast Off the Friendly Tea Pot; found toy part, sterling silver, Plexiglas **0857** Fisher Price Activity Center; toy parts, sterling silver **0858** The City Storyteller's Backpack; doll cabinet/wardrobe, supporting aluminum frame of old hiking bags, rope, various objects **0859** Ever So Much More So (Koons); Oil Paint on Christian Louboutin Pigalle **0860** The Girls in the Well; thrift store embroidery kit, embroidery thread **0861** The Fancy Lad; upholstery fabric samples, embroidery thread **0862** May Your Roots Go Down Deep into the Soil of God's Marvelous Love, or Steve and Lion; thrift store embroidery kit, embroidery thread **0863** Sad Sack and the Sugar Factory; thrift store embroidery kit, embroidery thread **0864** The Girls for the Well; thrift store embroidery kit, sewing scraps, embroidery thread **0865** Alaskan Starfish; plaster field jacket of an Edmontosaurus Hadrosaur humerus, plaster, ceramic **0866** Clem; various kitchen items: Jell-O molds, aluminum pans, spoons, forks, bullets, souvenir hat, wire, rivets, and screws **0867** Screach; various kitchen items: Jell-O mold, tin cans, spoons, forks, cabinet knobs, bottle caps, vegetable strainer parts, etc., wire, rivets, and screws **0868** Mechanical Violin Assemblage; violin, metal parts, found objects, natural coconut shell pieces, altered jewelry **0869** Hulamonkey; various kitchen items: Jell-O molds, cake mold, spoons, forks, rubicubes, broken salt shaker, wire, rivets, and screws **0870** Smiley One; various kitchen items: Jell-O mold, tin cans, spoons, forks, vegetable strainer, bottle caps, metal bowl, trinket, etc., wire, rivets, and screws **0871** Electric Chair; electrical hardware **0872** Kropokin and Kongo; old toy and computer parts **0873** Schalalala Fan Scarf Remix Collection; remixed wool fan scarves **0874** Child's Mandala; plastic bags and tape **0875** Flower Pop Mandala; plastic bags and tape **0876** Buymore Mandala; plastic bags and tape **0877** Mystery Mandala (detail); plastic bags and tape **0878** Consuming Conversation (A variant series of 200 cups); recycled tin cans, 10k gold, sterling silver; brass and silver handles, stainless-steel screws **0879** Consuming Conversation (A variant series of 200 cups); recycled tin cans, 10k gold, sterling silver; brass and silver handles, stainless-steel screws **0880** Consuming Conversation (A variant series of 200 cups); recycled tin cans, 10k gold, sterling silver; brass and silver handles, stainless-steel screws **0881** Indoor Longboard, 2008; embroidered upholstered vinyl, wooden deck, steel trucks, urethane wheels **0882** Inside Skate, 2006-08; upholstered vinyl, wooden deck, steel trucks, urethane wheels **0883** Consuming Conversation (A variant series of 200 cups); recycled tin cans, 10k gold, sterling silver; brass and silver handles, stainless-steel screws **0884** Burn It Up; fused and quilted found materials **0885** Mom; fused and quilted found materials **0886** Night is Young; fused and quilted found materials **0887** 101; fused and quilted found materials **0888** Innocence No.2; old plates with vintage/new and computer generated ceramic decals **0889** Never Kill a Mockingbird; old plates with vintage/new and computer generated ceramic decals **0890** Chicken Bones Frida; tin cans, chicken bones, repurposed beads and fabric, solvent, wire, game pieces, bottlecaps, Milagros **0891** Bliss; wood, blocks, recycled tin, photo, ephemera, nails **0892** Chewies Are Gooey; wood children's block, tin cans, tintype, nails **0893** Bird Dog; mixed media **0894** Blue Watch Dog; mixed media **0895** Dolly; mixed media **0896** Jane; mixed media **0897** Be (altered art doll); jewelry pieces and parts, lost earrings, heirloom broken treasures, brooches, charms, all recycled found objects **0898** Vision Board Collage; jewelry pieces and parts, lost earrings, heirloom broken treasures, brooches, charms, all recycled found objects **0899** Blk.Mas.Hero; photocopier transfer on Luan (disassembled chest of drawers), paint overlay, wooden craft letters; disassembled baby bed **0900** BOOKEND; repurposed vintage books **0901** Coke Head; plaster and coke cans **0902** Too Much Stuff #1: Unplugged; discontinued designer fabric samples (various fibers), organza, quilted, old electronics cables (metals, plastic), wood (lumber ends) **0903** I Saw the Light: A Tribute to Hank Williams; old light housing, golf tee, beads, candle holder, paint **0904** Stamp Rotator Machine; vintage postage stamps, nails, found stroller wheel, found buoy, found driftwood, vintage magnifying lenses **0905** Pan Am 707 Window Wall Art; authentic aluminum window salvaged from N880PA, a retired Pan Am 707 found in an Arizona scrapyard **0906** Kill Me or Make Me Beautiful; vintage porcelain with onglaze decoration, rope, wallpaper **0907** Deer Parade; slip cast porcelain, foam, found materials **0908** Twist Off;

bottlecaps and wire **0909** rdk; old floor lino mosaic **0910** Refocus room divider; film canisters, elastic **0910** Refocus room divider; film canisters, elastic **0911** Crustaceous Toddlerpede; plastic doll parts **0912** Footsey Toddlerpede; plastic doll parts **0914** Grub; woven street sweeper bristles and coffee stirrers cover a welded armature **0915** Half and Half Gourd; woven reclaimed street sweeper bristles and resawn hardwood scrap over a welded armature **0916** Weed Enclosure; bamboo sticks from an old kitchen blind **0917** My Little Alien; My Little Pony doll, Super Sculpey, wire, acrylic paint, varnish **0918** Cryptoscope; recycled camera parts **0919** Postmodem Discourse; reassembled chair pieces, appliance cord, bolt, foam donut, and discarded compact disc **0920** My Little Edward Scissorhands; My Little Pony doll, Super Sculpey, wire, metal, nylon, hair, acrylic paint, varnish **0921** Inside Skate, 2006–08; upholstered vinyl, wooden deck, steel trucks, urethane wheels **0922** Moss Graffiti; blended moss, buttermilk and sugar **0923** Cork Chair **0924** Measure of my Faith; wood box, wood canoe, Madonna, measuring tape **0925** Picture Perfect; used clothing, fabric, wood, foam, thread, yarn, embroidery floss, nails and screws **0926** Bugbot; cicada shell, resin, clockwork, found wood, electronic components **0927** Abundance: The Dawson City Trash Project **0928** Quitter; discarded cigarette packages filled with concrete, ink, acrylic **0929** Giant Quilt; discarded clothing **0930** Cycling Reality; found or reused oil drums, exercise bike, Rollerblade wheels, bike tires, bike chain, chainguard, right-angle motor shaft, pallet wood, steel **0931** Sculpture For Curling into a Ball on the Ground; recycled clothing, yarn **0932** Yokegrid #1; recycled t-shirts, thread **0933** Body Cavity Art; recycled clothing and bedding, thread, inflated plastic bags **0934** Body Cavity Art; recycled clothing and bedding, thread, inflated plastic bags **0935** Fly Me to The Moon; guitar, acrylic paint, sequins, paper, milagro, plastic angels, beads **0936** Snake Charmer; cable ties and aluminum conduit **0937** Art Deco; cable ties and aluminum conduit **0938** Concealer; recycled cosmetic container, needle-felted wool **0939** Faux-bidden; recycled cosmetic container, needle-felted wool **0940** Ceramixed Plate #0047; vintage porcelain with onglaze decoration **0941** Sunflower; porcelain and glass **0943** Border Town Girl #1; glass and paper beads, thread, laminated pulp fiction book cover **0944** Dead Man's Curves; glass beads,

playing card, mini playing cards, plastic toy, laminated lace, snake vertebrae, laminated pulp fiction book cover, cardboard pieces from spent fireworks, thread **0945** Particle Flow; glass beads, thread, laminated magazine cutouts taken from packing boxes **0946** Untitled; recycled plastic **0947** Lovebugs; found objects **0948** When It Snows, She Has No Fear for Her Household, for All of Them are Clothed in Scarlet; found boxes, PVC piping, fabrics with stitching and screen-printing **0949** Untitled (IC-63); refired industrial ceramic **0950** Tiki Love Truck – In memory of John Joe 'Ash' Amador **0951** Blissful Helix; 2,000 feet of retired chair-lift haul rope, salvaged structural steel, repurposed snowmaking pipe, hardware **0953** For Clemens; cable ties and screen **0954** Background Radiation; studio detritus (acrylic, plastics, foams) **0954** Studio Fragments (detail of background radiation); studio detritus (acrylic, plastics, foams) **0955** Juggernaut; porcelain and glass **0956** Environmental Thermostat; abandoned thermostat with miniature Zen garden, toothpick rake, and miniature forest **0956** Environmental Thermostat (detail); abandoned thermostat with miniature Zen garden, toothpick rake, and miniature forest **0957** Space; discarded plastic shopping bags and coiling foundation **0958** Sanctuary; discarded cardboard and fleece **0959** Memorial to Volant; 56 repurposed Volant stainless-steel skis, salvaged water pipe, hardware **0960** Call of the Wild; woven saplings **0961** Crossing Over; woven saplings **0962** Just For Looks; woven saplings **0963** So Inclined; woven saplings **0964** Miriello Grafico Letterwall; old channels letters from building signs, aluminum frame **0965** Yokegrid #2; recycled T-shirts, thread **0966** Pallet Sculptures and Glass Shard Tower; salvaged glass and pallets **0967** Postcards Recycled as Wallcovering **0968** Miriello Grafico lobby graphic; repurposed press sheets **0969** The Kitchen Door **0970** Postcards Recycled as Wallcovering **0971** Postcards Recycled as Wallcovering **0972** Queen Frostine Toy Cabinet; game boards, doll parts, doll clothes, toy parts **0973** Françoise; newsprint, fabric, ribbon, wood, spray paint **0974** The Doors Collections: Fusion Confusion and Juxtaposition; recycled door, place settings **0975** 907: 780 Chickens, 5 Cows, 18 Ducks, 2 Geese, 20 Pigs, 7 Rabbits, 29 Sheep, 46 Turkeys; dyed, recycled fabric, batting, sand, yarn, filament **0976** 18-Wheeler Wine Cellar; repurposed semi trailer **0977** reef; discarded and recycled plastics, clear plastic thread

and clear thumbtacks **0978** Snow Bowls for Ice Cream **0979** Ice and Snow Furniture Raised from Lake, or Frozeniture **0980** Larry Fox; 40 decommissioned lamp poles **0981** Diane; 60 decommissioned lamp poles, reused wire rope, hardware **0982** Giving Flight to Flightless Birds; dyed, recycled fabric, batting, sand, yarn, filament **0983** Indradhanush (Over the River Mersey); garments, steel, hardware **0984** s Warm; found objects **0984** s Warm (detail); found objects **0985** Water Wall; recycled water bottles filled with water **0986** Ribbons; cardboard, envelopes, print gocco **0987** Scarp; clothing borrowed from Goodwill **0987** Scarp (detail); clothing borrowed from Goodwill **0988** Sunt Omnes Unum (Latin: They are all one); garments, wood, steel **0989** Tribute; solid found garments **0990** Front of the Treatment Rooms; 50% recycled ceramic tiles **0991** The Art of Recycling—Harold Hill Library, UK; 70% recycled materials – including tiles, plastic toys, metal, pebbles, and mirror **0992** The Luis Ramirez Memorial Wall; 50% Recycled ceramic tiles, mosaics, and mixed media **0993** The Angola 3 & Kenny Zulu Whitmore Mural; 50% Recycled ceramic tiles and mosaics **0994** Canopy; garments **0995** Eden; garments, wood, wire, barricade mesh, hardware **0996** Spring, Sprang, Sprung; garments, ceiling brackets, paint and soundtrack **0997** The Good News Is, Recover Is Possible; slide mounts, found fabrics, strings **0998** The Nesting Habits of a Bumbershoot Lovebird that Dreamt of Flight...; oversized umbrella frame, discarded bamboo parasols, chopsticks, coffee stir stick, blinds, toothpicks, other found man-made and natural objects **0999** Artstream Nomadic Gallery; repurposed vintage Airstream trailer **1000** Because Whirl's After All; retired ladder, piano keys and hammers, collapsible gate, tennis rackets, crotchet hoops, Popsicle sticks, spools of thread

DIRECTORY OF CONTRIBUTORS

1mind1, Hungary
1mindegy@gmail.com
www.myspace.com/1mindegy
0233, 0441, 0520

2ReVert, Canada
2ReVert@gmail.com
www.2ReVert.com
0257, 0405, 0432, 0461

Dauvit Alexander, UK
gilmartin@justified-sinner.com
www.justified-sinner.com
0321, 0336, 0411, 0521

Jeff Alexander, Jalex Studios, USA
jalexstudios@entouch.net
www.jalexstudios.etsy.com
0696–0697, 0738, 0764, 0818, 0974

Thomas Allen, USA
thomasallenonline@gmail.com
www.thomasallenonline.com
0831–0835, 0900

Juliet Ames, The Broken Plate Pendant Co., USA
juliet@lbreakplates.com
www.lbreakplates.com
0323, 0360, 0433, 0503

Amuck, USA
ring@Amuckdesign.com
www.amuckdesign.com; www
.amuckdesign.blogspot.com
0465, 0468, 0471

Sylvia Anderson, USA
sylvia@SylviaAnderson.com
www.SylviaAnderson.com
0484

Angsty Teenage Eco Warriors, USA
0153, 0262, 0263

Curran Alexander Arnett, UK
curran_arnett@hotmail.co.uk
0554, 0558

Valerie Arntzen, Canada
arntval@telus.net
www.picasaweb.google.com/
valeriearntzen
0006, 0049, 0924

Camille Asseraf, USA
camileasseraf@gmail.com
www.paper-mode.com
0021, 0092

Miray Ataconli, Iilumi, Turkey
lilumi.design@gmail.com
www.lilumi.etsy.com
0320, 0402, 0457

Kristy Athens, USA
www.ithaka.etsy.com
0068, 0089

Jodie Atherton, Whitewater Ceramics, USA
jodie@whitewaterceramics.com
www.whitewaterceramics.com
0853, 0865

Atypyk, France
contact@atypyk
www.atypyk.com
0070, 0618, 0658

Stevie B., USA
stevieb@steviebjewelry.com
www.steviebjewelry.com
0415

Heather Bain, Canada
sisterbain@yahoo.com
0305, 0735, 0799

Lauren Baldwin, USA
laurenpbaldwin@gmail.com
www.web.me.com/breatheincolor
0364

Sarah Baldwin, USA
www.sarahmbaldwin.com
0948, 0997

Boris Bally, USA
boris@BorisBally.com
www.BorisBally.com
0681, 0699–0702, 0726, 0729, 0809

Kelly Basinger, USA
boxingday.etsy@gmail.com
www.shopboxingday.com
0494, 0814

Susan Beal, USA
www.westcoastcrafty.com
0638, 0647, 0650, 0790, 0791

Alana Beall, Vanity's Edge Design, USA
www.vanitysedgedesign.com
0824

Lauren Anabela Beaudoin, Creative Dexterity, USA
laurenanabela@gmail.com
www.creativedexterity.com
0317, 0545, 0547, 0551, 0602

Jon Beinart, Toddlerpedes, Australia
www.toddlerpedes.com
0911, 0912

David Benatan, Kozo Lamps, Israel
davidbenatan@gmail.com
www.kozo-lamp.com
0676, 0746, 0749

Rachel Chezlin Benefiel, USA
rachel@chezlin.com
www.chezlin.com
0231

Graham Bergh, Uncommon Goods, USA
0701, 0747

Brian Benfer, USA
brianbenfer@hotmail.com
www.brianbenfer.com
0949

Harriete Estel Berman, USA
bermaid@hattiete-estel-berman.info
www.harriete-estel-berman.info
0421, 0456, 0508, 0878–0880, 0883

Joshua Bienko, USA
joshuabienko@gmail.com
www.joshuabienko.com
0859

Kate Bingaman-Burt, USA
katebingamanburt@gmail.com
www.obsessiveconsumption.com
0112, 0296, 0304

Heather Lea Birdsall, Verdology, USA
heather@verdology.com
www.verdology.com
0041, 0043, 0045, 0067

Faith and Justina Blakeney, Compai Design Studio Inc., USA
compairehab@gmail.com
www.compai.com
0174, 0203, 0259

Hans Booy and Paulus Fugers, Germany
tulip.enterprises@gmail.com
www.tulip-enterprises.de
0906, 0940

Nick Bougas, USA
0090

Kat Bowes, Thistledown & Finch, USA
katbowes@hotmail.com
www.thistledownandfinch.etsy.com;
www.thistledownandfinch.blogspot.com
0218, 0307, 0311

Huw Briscoe, Unfold Studio, UK
huw@unfoldstudio.com
www.unfoldstudio.com
0099

Undine Brod, USA
www.undinebrod.com
0925

Heidi Brown, Heidala's, USA
heidalas_closet@yahoo.com
www.heidala.etsy.com
0251

Ian Brown, Australia
ianbrown4242@gmail.com
www.archivetwo.net
0605

Eva Buchala, Lady Artisan, USA
ebuchala@theladyartisan.com
www.ladyartisan.com
0003, 0073

Kim Buchheit, USA
kim@buchheitcreative.com
www.wildlywoolly.com; www
.buchheitcreative.com
0938–0939

Angus Mark Bungay, Canada
angusbungay@gmail.com
www.angusbungay.com
0901

Pamela Burns, Etcetrix, USA
etcetrix@etcetrix.com
www.etcetrix.com
0371, 0467, 0478, 0522

Anne Burton, USA
beantownhandmade@yahoo.com
www.beantownhandmade.etsy.com
0290

Laura Cahill, UK
cahill1020@hotmail.com
www.lauracahilldesigns.co.uk
0694, 0714–0716

Katy Campbell, ShutterKate, USA
contact@shutterkate.com
www.shutterkate.com
0216

Dustin Cantrell, USA
midnight26man@rocketmail.com
www.anomicbomb.blogspot.com
0524, 0560, 0567, 0594

Helen Carter, Secret Lentil, USA
helen@secretlentil.com
www.secretlentil.com
0117, 0213, 0239

Colleen Maria Casey, USA
www.SomeArtFabric.com
0127–0129, 0718, 0719, 0722

Maria Castrillo, Spain
castrillomaria@gmail.com
www.mariacastrillo.com
0396, 0443

Pattie Chalmers, USA
www.pattiechalmers.com
0860–0864

Jarod Charzewski, USA
Jarodcharzewski@hotmail.com
www.jarodcharzewski.com
0987

Christie Chase, USA
www.christiechase.etsy.com
0703

Chica and Jo, USA
chicaandjo@chicaandjo.com
www.chicaandjo.com
0273, 0687

Sally Chinea, UK
sally-chinea@hotmail.co.uk
0946

Elaine G. Chu, USA
egc@egchu.com
www.egchu.com
0009, 0069

Christine Claringbold, Eye Pop Art, USA
eyepopart@yahoo.com
www.eyepopart.etsy.com
0442, 0492, 0649, 0654, 0727

Randall Cleaver, USA
randallcleaver@aol.com
0668, 0704, 0766

Robyn L. Coburn, Iggy Jingles Crafts, USA
dezignarob@gmail.com
www.iggyjingles.blogspot.com
0272, 0310

Merill Comeau, USA
14thebeesknees@gmail.com
www.merillcomeau.com
0121–0124

Chandra L. Corcoran, USA
ChandraLC@hotmail.com
www.c2design.etsy.com
0806, 0812

Cindy Cordero-Stout, UK
0383, 0464

Adam Patrick Easter Cottingham, USA
cerebro21@gmail.com
0632, 0774

Mary Ellen Coumerilh, USA
maryellen@maryzoom.com
www.maryzoom.com
0252

David Craft, GoGreenCraft, USA
Coolhats@live.com
www.davescoolhats.com; www
.gogreencraft.com
0189, 0243, 0253, 0299, 0586, 0587,
0590, 0591

Heather Crossley, Australia
mkhc@powerup.com.au
www.homepage.powerup.com
.au/~mkhc
0079

Mandy Curl, Mandinka Designs, USA
mandinkadesigns@comcast.net
www.mandinka.etsy.com
0154–0159

Cynthia Murray Design, USA
landscapejewel@yahoo.com
www.Flickr.com/photos/landscapejewel
0316

Dana Damm,
Thomasina Jewelry, USA
thomasinajewelry@yahoo.com
www.thomasinajewelry.com
0416, 0476, 0504

Misty Darrington,
Gemmabeads, USA
GemmaBeads@gmail.com
www.gemmabeads.blogspot.com
0358, 0389, 0447, 0485

Drék Davis, USA
rodrecas@gmail.com
www.flickr.com/photos/
postmodempixenflix/; www.cafepress
.com/Durtees
0899, 0919

Jeff Davis, Vinylux, USA
records@vinylux.net
www.vinylux.net
0652, 0688, 0813

Merliyn DeGraaf, Julia de
Jong, and Mieke Fokkinga,
The Netherlands
MMF@s4all.nl
www.miekemaaike.nl; www.juliaja.nl
0969

Guerra de la Paz, USA
www.guerradelapaz.com
0983, 0988, 0989, 0994–0996

Renee de Sibour, My Ugly
Kitty, USA
renee@myuglykitty.com
www.myuglykitty.com
0048, 0354

Gil Delapointe and Pierre Andre
Senizergues, USA
info@skatestudyhouse.com
www.skatestudyhouse.com
0705, 0753, 0785, 0800, 0808

Kim Depenbrok, KD Design
Studio, USA
kimkdep@aol.com
www.kimkdep.etsy.com; www
.KDDesignStudio.blogspot.com
0337, 0362

Design Stories, Sweden
kerstin@designstories.se
www.designstories.se
0625, 0678, 0730, 0756, 0759

Christine Dhein, USA
christinedhein@yahoo.com
www.christinedheim.com
0324, 0327, 0437, 0593, 0600

Liz Dickey, 1.by.liz, USA
1.by.liz@gmail.com
www.1byliz.etsy.com
0617, 0629, 0744, 0745, 0788, 0792

Lauren Donnelly, Paperelle, USA
LEDonnelly@gmail.com
www.paperelle.etsy.com
0322, 0496

Patrick Dougherty, USA
stickwork@earthlink.net;
branchwork@earthlink.net
www.stickwork.net
0960–0963

Ami Drach and Dov
Ganchrow, Israel
amidov@netvision.net.il
www.amidov.com
0817, 0821, 0826, 0828

Jessie Driscoll, Made
From Coins, USA
jessie@madefromcoins.com
www.madefromcoins.com
0369, 0376, 0377

Sandy Drobny, USA
sdrobny1@aol.com
0109, 0115, 0149, 0196, 0283, 0284

Didi Dunphy, USA
dididunphy@modernconvenience.com
www.modernconvenience.com
0881–0882, 0921

Susan Dwyer, Up in the Air
Somewhere, USA
www.upintheairsomewhere.com
0002, 0004, 0005

David Edgar, Plastiquarium, USA
dallenedgar@gmail.com
www.plastiquarium.com
0842–0847

Mary Engel, USA
maryeengel@gmail.com
www.maryengel.net
0893–0896

englishcookies, UK
englishcookies@yahoo.fr
www.englishcookies.etsy.com
0789

Etti & Otti's Oddments by
Michelle Biscotti, USA
BadaBingVintage@aol.com
www.EttiandOttisOddments.etsy.com
0398

Jessi Eurich, Ruby Studios, USA
rubystudios3@gmail.com
www.rubystudios.etsy.com
0523

Mandy Fariello, USA
farstar1310@verizon.net
www.flickr.com/photos/farstarr; www
.farstarr.blogspot.com; www.farstarr
.etsy.com
0026, 0215

Christine Farnan, USA
Chris51496@aol.com
0682

Raul Siro Ferreira, USA
clothesmaker@sirodesign.com
www.sirodesign.com
0161–0163, 0165, 0166

Amanda Fiedler, USA
alfieds@gmail.com
www.amandafiedler.com
0776

Ruth Fiege, USA
wegerjohn@msn.com
0014, 0035, 0050, 0052, 0062

virginia fleck, USA
info@virginiafleck.com
www.virginiafleck.com
0874–0877

Amy Rubin Flett, Canada
info@theforgottenthings.com
www.theforgottenthings.com
0020, 0904, 0913

Ken Flett, Canada
kenflett@gmail.com
www.kenflett.com; www.rustystories
.blogspot.com
0083, 0542, 0574, 0909

Julie Floersch, USA
julie@juliefloersch.com
www.juliefloersch.com
0171

JoyAnn Flowers,
Joya Jewelry, USA
joyajewelry@hotmail.com
www.joyajewelry.etsy.com
0350, 0355, 0505

Maggie French, USA
maggiemay1973@hotmail.com
www.maggiefrenchfolkart.etsy.com
0666

Nancy Gamon, USA
nancy_gamon@hotmail.com
www.nancygamon.com
0140, 0268, 0269, 0271, 0723

Tammy Gay, Canada
myjunck@sympatico.ca
www.junck.etsy.com
0399, 0474, 0481

GGrippo, trash-à-porter, USA
info@nydesignroom.com
www.ggrippo.com
0235, 0256, 0302, 0314, 0811

Gi and Pindo, USA
info@giandpindo.com
www.giandpindo.com
0370, 0428, 0430

Jami Gigot and Nicolas Worth,
The Grateful Thread Ltd., UK
jaminico@the-gratefulthread.com
www.the-gratefulthread.com
0436, 0731

Diane Gilleland,
CraftyPod, USA
diane@deepideas.com
www.craftypod.com
0012, 0038, 0047, 0058

Annika Ginsberg,
Mahka Craft, USA
www.MahkaCrafts.blogspot.com
0132, 0294

Girl Industries, UK
Katy@girlindustries.com
www.girlindustries.etsy.com
0019

Heather Goldberg, USA
heather.goldberg@gmail.com
www.PetitOiseau.etsy.com
0626, 0642, 0670, 0689

Ian Gonsher, USA
gonsherdesign@hotmail.com
www.gonsherdesign.com
0651

Alicia Goodwin, USA
lingua.nigra@gmail.com
www.linguanigra.com
0502

Jann Greenland, USA
jupiter@jannland.com
0660, 0778

Alina Gridley, Silver Garden, USA
alina@atlantisfusedglass.net
www.SilverGarden.etsy.com
0357

Cary Ann Grimm, Studio (RE),
USA
carygrimm@mac.com
0315

Virginia Griswold, USA
virginiagriswold@yahoo.com
www.virginiagriswold.com
0622, 0941, 0955

Sam Gueydon and Friends, USA
sgueydon@att.net
0571

Jylian Gustlin, USA
jylian@acutedelirium.com
www.jyliangustlin.com
0086, 0088, 0093, 0094

Jeannette Gutierrez, USA
jlg10_guard-spm@yahoo.com
0359, 0519

Ryan Habbyshaw, USA
ryan@habbyshaw.com
www.habbyshaw.com
0717

Michelle Hansen, Undone
Clothing, USA
www.undoneclothing.etsy.com
0160, 0169, 0285

John Hardin, Tin Can
Luminary, USA
tincanluminary@yahoo.com
www.myspace.com/tincanluminary
0633, 0644, 0675, 0707

Jenny Hart, USA
www.sublimestitching.com
0306

Michelle Hartney,
Recycled Rings, USA
michelle@recycledrings.com
www.recycledrings.com
0412, 0459, 0501

Patti Haskins, USA
phaskins@swbell.net
www.pattihaskins.com
0967, 0970, 0971

Becky Hawley, USA
becky@beckydesigns.com
www.beckydesigns.etsy.com; www
.beckydesigns.com
0030, 0032, 0076

Juliet Heil, Greener Landz, USA
greenerlandz@live.com
www.greenerlandz.com
0641, 0673

Mae Henry, USA
shipwreck.eureka@gmail.com
www.maehenry.etsy.com;
www.shipwreck-shop.com
0191

heybales, USA
heybales@yahoo.com
0667, 0690

Janet Hickey, USA
janet@janethickey.com
www.janethickey.com
0784

Randy Hill, Art Foundango, USA
artfoundango@gmail.com
www.artfoundango.com
0903, 0935

Megan K. Hoffman, Frank &
Gertrude, The Netherlands
frankandgertrude@gmail.com
www.frankandgertrude.com
0011, 0015, 0017, 0054

Bland Hoke, USA
blandhoke@gmail.com
www.blandhoke.com
0951, 0959, 0980, 0981

Danielle Holke, Canada
danielle_holke@sympatico.ca
www.lilyonthedustbin.com;
www.knithacker.com;
www.lilydustbin.etsy.com
0404, 0417, 0453, 0513

Chery Holmes, Canada
chery@ca.inter.net
0422, 0455, 0463, 0489

Bryant Holsenbeck, USA
www.bryantholsenbeck.com
0836–0839, cover and title page art

Jeremy T. Howard, USA
germicidal@gmail.com
www.germicidalink.com
0563, 0566

Will Hunt, Australia
willhuntdesign@gmail.com
0611

Stanton Hunter, USA
sschh@earthlink.net
www.stantonhunter.com
0956, 0966

Annada Hypes, Token Emotion, USA
abushorn00@yahoo.com
www.tokenemotion.etsy.com
0499, 0758

Patrizia Iacino, Globalcoolo Jewelry, USA
jewelry@globalcoolo.com
jewelry@globalcoolo.com
0420, 0424

Janelle Iglesias, USA
janelleiglesias@yahoo.com
www.LasHermanasIglesias.com
0977, 0998, 1000

Emu Izaki, New Zealand
www.flickr.com/photos/mamephotos
0120, 0185, 0244, 0277, 0292

Julee Dunekacke Jaeger, USA
juleejaeger@gmail.com
www.juleedunekacke.com
0223, 0242, 0301, 0556, 0557, 0596

Anneke Jakobs, The Netherlands
info@annekejakobs.nl
www.annekejakobs.nl
0827

Teresa Jessee, 2birds1stone, USA
tjjessee@gmail.com
0672

Connie Jeung-Mills, USA
0008

Jeff Johnson, USA
jeffhojo3@earthlink.net
www.jeffjohnsonstudio.com
0538

Dan Jones, Tinkerbots, USA
jedi65@peoplepc.com
www.flickr.com/tinkerbots
0541, 0562, 0564, 0569, 0584, 0585

Thomas P. Jones, USA
webmaster@nuyakacreek.com
www.nuyakacreek.com
0976

Wendy Jordan, USA
wendy_jordan@yahoo.com
0056, 0074

Claire Joyce, USA
joyceclaire@hotmail.com
www.clairejoyce.com
0131, 0194, 0209

Matt Joyce, NYCResistor, USA
matt@nycresistor.com
www.music-piracy.com
0579

Tom Kabat, Woodenbikes, USA
tomkabat@aol.com
www.woodenbikes.com
0568, 0576, 0582

Mari Kasurinen, Finland
spippo_@hotmail.com
www.marikasurinen.com
0917, 0920

Michelle Kaufmann, USA
www.michellekaufmann.com; www
.blog.michellekaufmann.com
0612, 0648, 0797, 0985

Margaux Kent, The Black Spot Books, USA
theblackspot@mac.com
www.theblackspotbooks.com
0435

Walter Kent, The Black Spot Books, USA
theworldinpastel@yahoo.com
0615

Ai Kijima, USA
ai@aikijima.com
www.aikijima.com
0884–0887

Gege Kingston, USA
0431, 0517

Lisa Kirkpatrick, Australia
estasketch@gmail.com
www.estasketch.etsy.com
0059–0061

Megan Klepp, Ta-Dah, USA
mklepp@yahoo.com
www.tadahpdx.com
0071, 0695

Josh Korwin & Alyssa Zukas, notschlock, USA
josh@threestepsahead.com
www.notschlock.com
0535

Aaron Kramer, Urban Objects, USA
urbanobjects@gmail.com
www.urban-objects.com
0677, 0683, 0708, 0914, 0915, 0923

Randall Kramer, USA
randall@kramerdesignstudio.com
www.kramerdesignstudio.com
0656, 0657, 0674, 0698, 0796

Rene Kreis, USA
rkreis@gmail.com
www.florigander.etsy.com
0114, 0603

Alison Lait, Canada
alisonlait@hotmail.com
www.sewnagain.etsy.com
0312

Margaux Lange, USA
www.margauxlange.com
0343–0348

Jeaneé Ledoux, Honeydoux, USA
jeanee@honeydoux.com
www.honeydoux.com
0408

Jeanée Ledoux, Re-Construct DVD, USA
jeanee@honeydoux.com
www.reconstructdvd.com
0767

Whitney Lee, USA
whitney@whitneyleephotography.com
www.whitneyleephotography.com;
www.madewithsweetlove.com
0848–0852

Janet Lee, Janet Planet Designs, Canada
jml@teraplanning.com
www.janetplanet.com; www
.janetplanetdesigns.blogspot.com
0080–0082

Runa Leo and Jon Marín, Spain
runaleo@yahoo.de
www.leocollage.sebjo.de
0628

Max Liboiron, USA
maxliboiron@gmail.com
www.maxliboiron.com
0927

Keith Linton, USA
dklintonart@yahoo.com
0954

David Lipson, Lipson Robotics, USA
DLipson1@yahoo.com
www.lipsonrobotics.com
0559, 0561, 0598, 0601

Lisa Orgler Design, USA
lisaorgler@huxcomm.net
www.lisaorglerdesign.blogspot.com
0151, 0512

Alan Lishness, USA
0565

LOOM STUDIO, USA
ralph@loomstudio.com
www.loomstudio.com
0760

Kristin Lora, USA
kristin@kristinlora.com
www.kristinlora.com
0426, 0537, 0549, 0597, 0599

Sayraphim Lothian, Australia
her@sayraphimlothian.com
www.sayraphimlothian.com
0918

Emily Machovec, USA
emach177@kutztown.edu
0750

Airdrie Makim, Australia
airdrie@joolz.com.au
www.joolz.com.au
0325. 0479

Priya Mani, Denmark
email@priyamani.com
www.priyamani.com
0136, 0274, 0300

Betty Maple, USA
betty.maple@gmail.com
0232

Ashley Markus, Off the Hooks, Canada
offthehookscrafts@gmail.com
www.offthehooks.etsy.com
0313

Josie Marsh, Wooly Baby, USA
info@wooly-baby.com
www.wooly-baby.com
0236, 0270, 0308, 0309

Guylaine & Isabelle Martineau, .tomate d'épingles, Canada
info@tomatedepingles.ca
www.tomatedepingles.ca
0429

Matthew Laumann Design, USA
MatthewLaumann@gmail.com
www.MATTHEWLAUMANN.com
0072

Iain McCaig, UK
imccaig@gmail.com
0592

Terry and Mary McCoy, Inoudid's Attic, USA
inoudidsattic@yahoo.com
www.inoudidsattic.etsy.com
0805

Ryan "Zieak" McFarland, USA
zieak@mitkof.org
www.zieak.com
0525, 0527, 0823

Clay McLaurin, USA
claymcla@gmail.com
www.alisonwilder.com
0623, 0624, 0820, 0822, 0825

Julie McNiel, USA
www.jmcniel.com/eureka
0016, 0077, 0097, 0101

Alleghany Meadows, USA
alleghanym@gmail.com
www.art-stream.com
0999

MeanBean, USA
kristinleamy@hotmail.com
www.mymeanbean.com
0183, 0222, 0224, 0289

Gaye Medbury, USA
stmpbabe@insightbb.com
0446, 0451, 0815

Brianna Meli, Melt Brianna, USA
xstraycatx@sbcglobal.net
www.meltbrianna.etsy.com
0264, 0287

Lee Meredith, Leethal, USA
leemeredith@gmail.com
www.leethal.net
0130, 0134, 0182, 0249, 0250

Cat Merrick, USA
Cat@CatMerrick.com
www.catmerrick.com
0775, 0780, 0781

Ron Miriello, Miriello Grafico, Inc., USA
ron@miriellografico.com
www.miriellografico.com
0964, 0968

Iris Mishly Polymer Clay Art, Israel
imishly@gmail.com
www.arcoiris.co.il; www.polymerionline
.blogspot.com
0427

Mitchell Glassworks, USA
Linda@MitchellGlassworks.com
www.MitchellGlassworks.com
0622, 0819

Audrey Molinare, Erin Burke, and Danielle Benson, USA
www.dootdot.com
0973, 0986

Juliette Montague and Greg Stange, USA
letters@stangmont.com
www.stangmount.com; www
.stangmontdesign.com
0866, 0867, 0869, 0870

Elizabeth Lundberg Morisette, USA
elmorisette@gmail.com
www.elmorisette.blogspot.com
0146, 0147, 0684, 0908

Mr. Spunky, UK
0872, 0950, 0990–0993

Kirsten Muenster, USA
info@kirstenmuenster.com
www.kirstenmuensterjewelry.com
0497

Shannon Mulkey, Patina, USA
shannon@ilovepatina.com
www.ilovepatina.com
0118, 0119, 0148, 0164, 0211, 0246

Heather Youghdahl Mullins, USA
relevantreuse@gmail.com
www.relevantreuse.etsy.com; www
.heathermullins.com
0150, 0930, 0930

Lucas Muñoz and David Tamane, enPieza! eStudio, Spain
enpieza@enpieza.com
www.enpieza.com
0621, 0655, 0737, 0765, 0779

Richard Nagy,
Datamancer.net, USA
Datamancer@Datamancer.net
www.Datamancer.net
0528, 0536, 0570, 0609, 0610

Laurel Nathanson, USA
laurelnathanson@yahoo.com
www.laurelnathanson.com
0053, 0095, 0810, 0856, 0857, 0972

Navarro Vineyards, USA
sales@navarrowine.com
www.navarrowine.com
0640

Lara Newsom,
Handmade Pretties, USA
thepretties@handmadepretties.com
www.handmadepretties.com;
www.handmadepretties.etsy.com
0201, 0260, 0807, 0830

Nifty Thrifty, UK
tracey.benton@talktalk.net
www.nifty-thrifty.com
0107, 0221

Helen Nodding, Australia
princessnodding@hotmail.com
www.storiesfromspace.co.uk
0916, 0922

Bree Norlander,
Hot Tea Apparel, USA
hotteaapparel.blogspot.com
0645

Bryan Northrup, USA
bryan@biolumglass.com
www.biolumglass.com
0706, 0801

NottyPooch Design, Malaysia
huey@nottypooch.com
www.nottypooch.etsy.com
0110, 0254, 0255, 0258

Irina Nunez, USA
irina_nunez@hotmail.com
www.creativebabies.etsy.com
0187, 0188, 0190, 0202, 0225, 0282

Linda and Opie O'Brien, USA
gourdart@burntofferings.com
www.burntofferingws.com
0445, 0890–0892

Odelia Makes Dolls, Israel
odelia_l@email.com
www.odelialavie.com
0126, 0192

Annie O'Kane, USA
clubmarival@yahoo.com
0487

Constance Old, co. inc., USA
cdold@optonline.net
0748, 0761, 0770, 0777

Monika Olejnik, Canada
mo.origindesigns@gmail.com
0635

Sarah Olmstead, USA
www.punkbrewsters.blogspot.com
0619, 0782

Ouissi, British Cream Tea, UK
ouissi@britishcreamtea.co.uk
www.britishcreamtea.co.uk
0180, 0181

OutsaPop Trashion, Finland
outsapop.com@gmail.com
www.outsapop.com
0440

Edie Joanna Overturf, USA
www.edieoverturf.com
0339, 0353, 0514

Henry H. Owings, Chunklet
Graphic Control, USA
henry@chunklet.com
www.chunklet.com
0543, 0548, 0550, 0604

Sarah Hayes Owings, USA
0724

Jenn Parnell and
Sherri Shawver, USA
0506

Nicholas Martin Paul, USA
nickpaul@gmail.com
www.nickpaul.com
0526, 0540, 0693, 0804

Mary-Jo Peritore,
MerCurios, USA
melios@gmail.com;
info@mercurios.net
www.mercurios.etsy.com
0388, 0449

Matt Perry, USA
mattperry43@gmail.com
0539, 0588, 0589

Sarah Perry, USA
vegsar@hotmail.com
0205

Brian Peters & Daphne Firos, USA
www.designlabworkshop.com
0653

Christy Petterson, a bardis, USA
hello@abardis.com
www.abardis.com
0042

Hilary Pfeifer, USA
www.hilarypfeifer.com; www
.bunnywithatoolbelt.com
0947, 0984

Caitlin Phillips,
Rebound Design, USA
cphillips@rebound-designs.com
www.rebound-designs.com
0113, 0226–0230

Jane Pierce, zJayne, USA
zjayne@gmail.com
www.zJayne.com; www.zJayne.etsy.com
0897, 0898

Laura Hawker Plouzek,
Xoelle, USA
elle@xoelle.com
www.xolelle.com
0133, 0139, 0802, 0829

Jessica Plymate, Aorta Apparel,
USA
jwpbot@yahoo.com
www.aortaapparel.com
0105, 0141–0145

Pouch, UK
contact@pouchbags.co.uk
www.pouchbags.co.uk
0152, 0212, 0288, 0295, 0298

Cristina Poulopoulou, Greece
karmologyclinic@gmail.com
www.karmologyclinic.wordpress.com
0111, 0220

Laura Prentice, USA
laura.prentice@gmail.com
www.flickr.com/photos/lauraprentice
0929

Amanda Preske, USA
beadworkbyamanda@gmail.com
www.beadworkbyamanda.blogspit.com
0529–0534

Heather Price,
Winemakerssister, USA
winemakerssister@yahoo.com
www.winemakerssister.etsy.com; www
.winemakerssister.artfire.com; www
.winemakerssister.blogspot.com
0065, 0066, 0208

Holly Priester, Blue Fish Moon
Studios, USA
holly@bluefishmoon.com
www.bluefishmoon.com
0469, 0470

Michelle Pugh, Smashgirl
Mosiacs, USA
smashgirl84@gmail.com
www.smashgirl.etsy.com
0007–0010

Amy Quarry, Canada
thefrontroom@gmail.com
www.amyquarry.ca
0197–0200

Anna Raddatz, USA
annaraddatz@gmail.com
www.anagramworkshop.etsy.com
0116, 0241

Sean Michael Ragan, USA
sean@seanmichaelragan.com
www.seanmichaelragan.com
0743, 0757

Michele Rappoport,
Blingaling, USA
blingaling@cox.net
www.blingaling.etsy.com
0516

Katherine Rasmussen,
Reiter8, USA
info@reiter8.com
www.reiter8.com
0135, 0138, 0167, 0173, 0772

Reestore Ltd., UK
max@reestore.com
www.reestore.com
0613, 0616

Carrie Reichardt aka
The Baroness, UK
0888, 0889, 0950, 0990–0993

Gustav Reyes,
Simply Wood Rings, USA
craftsman@simplywoodrings.com
www.simplywoodrings.com
0380–0382, 0386

Molly B. Right, USA
moboright@comcast.net
www.mollybright.com
0055, 0057

Meg J. Roberts, USA
robertsmj@vcu.edu
0957, 0958

Jen Roder, Rotorcaps, USA
jen@jenroder.com
www.rotorcaps.com
0333, 0356, 0395, 0509

Sonya Coulson Rook, USA
mail@metamorphosismetals.com
www.metamorphosismetals.com
0330, 0378, 0379, 0385

Velma Root,
Colorbomb Creations, USA
velma@colorbombcreations.com
www.colorbombcreations.com
0193, 0247, 0248, 0261

Jim Rosenau, USA
jim@thisintothat.com
www.thisintothat.com
0627, 0630, 0631

Joyce Rosenfeld, USA
joyce.rosenfeld@gmail.com
0001, 0029

Jesse Rutherford,
Bent-Tronics, USA
jr@bent-tronics.com
www.bent-tronics.com
0544, 0578, 0606

Sandra Salamony, USA
sandranoel@aol.com
www.SandraSalamony.com
0367, 0373, 0721

Amy M. Santoferraro, USA
santoferraro@yahoo.com
www.mysanto.com
0643, 0907

Andres Savi, Estonia
andres@kalmetu.vil.ee
0607

Ben Schachter, USA
schach1000@aol.com
www.benschachter.com
0871, 0936, 0937, 0953

Diane Schamp, USA
dianesdangles@peoplespc.com
www.dianesdangles.artfire.com
0500

Rüdiger Schlömer, Germany
info@schalalala.de
www.schalalala.de
0873

Jiskar Schmitz, The Netherlands
www.jiskar.nl
0553, 0555, 0572

Andrea Schneeberg, USA
andreaschneeberg70@hotmail.com
andreaschneeberg.googlepages.com
0217, 0245, 0685

Idolly schwendener, Canada
ldolly@gmail.com
www.isdesigns.etsy.com
0671, 0768

Sally Seamans, Tin Can Sally, USA
tincansally@yahoo.com
www.sallyseamans.com
0840, 0841

Secret Leaves Paperworks, USA
inquire@secretleaves.com
www.secretleaves.com
0024

Holland Seydel and Eliav Nissan,
Haute Nature, USA
seydel_h@hotmail.com
www.hautenature.blogspot.com
0170, 0634, 0712

Betsy Sibor, Foxglove
Accessories, USA
foxgloveaccessories@gmail.com
www.foxgloveaccessories.com
0340, 0352, 0413

Amanda Siska,
Bread and Badger, USA
amanda@breadandbadger.com
www.breadandbadger.com
0711, 0725, 0733, 0736, 0739, 0771

Susan Carlson Skalak, USA
0237, 0297

Steven Smith, Thabto Ltd., UK
steve@thabto.co.uk
www.thabto.co.uk
0751

Vanda Sousa, Portugal
vanda.f.sousa@sapo.pt
www.vandasousasnapshots
.blogspot.com
0732, 0816

SpoonerZ, USA
rachellefallon@yahoo.com
www.SpoonerZ.biz
0363, 0409, 0450

Robyn Sprung, USA
robyn.sprung@gmail.com
0372, 0452, 0482, 0483, 0515

Becky Stern, USA
becky@sternlab.org
www.sternlab.org
0486, 0552, 0583, 0595, 0663

Taylor Cass Stevenson, USA
redsemilla@riseup.net
www.redsemillaroja.org
0763

stiksel, The Netherlands
mail@stiksel.nl
www.stiksel.nl
0303

**Windy Wise Stiner,
The Petticoat Pirate,** USA
sun2ssoil@aol.com
www.thepetticoatpirate.com
0125, 0276

Stuart Karten Design, USA
info@kartendesign.com
www.kartendesign.com
0691, 0786

Studio Cherie, USA
Cherie@StudioCherie.com
www.StudioCherie.com
0662

Krista Stumph, Canada
kristastumph@mac.com
www.web.mac.com/kristastumph
0018, 0022, 0028, 0031, 0034, 0078

Teresa Sullivan, USA
beadnutz66@yahoo.com; info@
teresasullivanstudio.com
www.teresasullivanstudio.com
0349, 0493, 0854, 0855, 0943–0945

Sayaka Suzuki, USA
sayaka.bean@gmail.com; suzukis@
vcu.edu
www.sayaka.-suzuki.com
0975, 0982

**Sweater Hospital by
fibrevolution,** USA
fibrevolution@gmail.com
www.SweaterHospital.etsy.com; www
.thefibrevolution.com
0219, 0234, 0240, 0291

Ted Swiet, USA
tedswiet@gmail.com
www.tedswiet.com
0679, 0734

**Stephanie Syjuco,
Anti-Factory,** USA
www.anti-factory.com
0137, 0207, 0214, 0265, 0275

Corinne Okada Takara, USA
corinne@okadadesign.com
www.okadadesign.com
0039, 0084, 0184

Take Off Your Clothes, USA
takeoffyourclothesetsy@gmail.com
www.takeoffyourclothes.etsy.com
0206

Kim Taylor, The Sassy Crafter,
USA
sassycrafter@gmail.com
www.sassycrafter.com
0636, 0637, 0664, 0669, 0720, 0793

**Shawn Taylor, P
RASSEIN DESIGN STUDIO,** USA
niayasmama@yahoo.com; shawn@
prasseindesignstudio.com
www.prasseindesignstudio.etsy.com
0387, 0390, 0391, 0394

**Rebecca Tegtmeyer, Sown
Designs,** USA
www.sowndesigns.com
0639, 0686, 0709, 0783

Christine Terrell, Adaptive Reuse,
USA
christine@adaptivereuser.com
www.adaptivereuser.com
0400, 0460

Tiffany Teske, Canada
tiffany@oldsage.com
www.tiffanyteske.blogspot.com
0414, 0438, 0659, 0661, 0762

**Valerie Thai, CABIN + CUB
DESIGN,** Canada
valerie@cabinandcub.com
www.cabinandcub.com; www.cabin
.etsy.com
0037, 0063, 0064, 0100

**The CityStorytellers, Very
Serious Urban Storytelling
Society,** The Netherlands
faiz@faizzohri.com
www.faizzohri.com
0858

Nancy Smythe Thompson, USA
sassafrascreations@mindspring.com
www.sassafrascreations.com
0406, 0507, 0511

**Tiffany Threadgould,
RePlayGround,** USA
moreinfo@replayground.com
www.replayground.com
0710, 0713, 0740, 0910

Kathy Tibbets, USA
ktibbits@lrec.org
www.fluffyscompleatbouti.etsy.com
0868

Erwin Timmers, USA
erwin@washglass.com
www.ecoartglass.com
0755, 0769, 0798, 0803

Judy Titche, Rezoom, USA
Rezoom123@live.com
www.Rezoom.etsy.com
0175, 0176, 0266, 0267, 0773

Beth Todd, USA
www.BethToddCreatz.etsy.com;
www.BethToddDesigns.com
0392, 0458, 0462, 0794

**Ward Wallau, Milan Micich,
Tokens & Icons,** USA
milan@tokens-icons.com
www.tokens-icons.com
0331, 0366, 0384, 0401, 0434, 0701,
0905

**Monica Topping,
Rock Chick Designs,** USA
rokchike@gmail.com
www.rokchike.etsy.com
0439, 0444

Steve Travis, USA
creativeguys@mac.com
www.dragonflyhill.org
0580

Jeanne Tremel, USA
jmariet000@hotmail.com
www.workingforpeanuts.etsy.com
0096

Alice Trumbull, USA
trumbam@hotmail.com
www.thepuddlepeople.com
0665, 0728

Bob Turek, USA
boburekdesign@gmail.com
www.coroflot.com/bobturek
0573, 0575

**Wendy Uhlman, Industrial
Designer,** USA
wendyuhlman@yahoo.com
www.unit2.us
0741, 0742

John T. Unger, USA
john@johntunger.com
www.johntunger.com
0085, 0087, 0577, 0581

Elke Ursin, Sweet Twee Lab, USA
sweettweelab@gmail.com
www.sweettweelab.etsy.com; www.
sweettweelab.blogspot.com
0013

Lauren Venell, Sweet Meats, USA
info@sweet-meats.com
www.sweet-meats.com
0177–0179, 0293

Amalia Versaci, USA
amalia@amaliaversaci.com
www.amaliaversaci.com
0342, 0410, 0787

Sarah-Maria Vischer, USA
smvphotography@hotmail.com
www.burdastyle.com/member/
smvphotography
0238, 0429

Francesca Vitali, USA
fruccidesign@gmail.com
www.fruccidesign.etsy.com
0318, 0335, 0338, 0365, 0454, 0491

Derek von Essen, Canada
www.derekvonessen.ca
0928

Kelly Wakefield-Beytia, USA
tresijas.design@yahoo.com
www.tresijas.etsy.com
0319

Rebecca Ward, Australia
rebeccawardjewellery@optusnet
.com.au
www.rebeccawardjewellery.com
0368, 0397, 0403, 0407, 0418, 0423

Helena Wehrstein, Canada
helaweh@hotmail.com
0902, 0952

**Jessi C. Welch, Cheap Date
Jewelry,** USA
cheapdatejewelry@gmail.com
www.cheapdatejewelry.etsy.com
0495, 0498

**Brian Western, Western Art
Glass,** USA
westernartglass@yahoo.com
www.westernartglass.etsy.com
0393, 0620, 0646

Whit McLeod Furniture, USA
info@whitmcleod.com
www.whitmcleod.com
0614, 0752, 0754

Alison Wilder, USA
aw339@bard.edu
www.alisonwilder.com
0023, 0931–0934, 0965

Valerie William, Additions, USA
additionsstyle@sbcglobal.net
www.additions.etsy.com; www
.additions.1000markets.com
0341, 0374, 0375, 0466

Cynthia Williams, USA
pdxcyn@yahoo.com
0361, 0419, 0473, 0490

**Kathryn Wilson, Junkhouse
Dollyard Designs,** Japan
ryndollyn@gmail.com
www.junkhousedollyard.com
0102–0104, 0106, 0168, 0210

Lisa Winter, USA
jlwinter@sbcglobal.net
www.winterdreams.etsy.com
0286

Dustin Wood, Hanger3, USA
mail@hanger3.com
www.hanger3.com
0328, 0329, 0332, 0680

Alicia L. Woods, USA
0108, 0692, 0795

Carroll M. Woods, USA
carroods@aol.com
www.flickr.com/photos/
dumpsterdiversanonymous
0025, 0033, 0036, 0075, 0098, 0186

**Brenda B. Wright,
Bowenwright Crafts LC,** USA
bbwright98@aol.com
www.bowenwright.com
0475, 0480, 0510, 0518

Christina L. Wright, USA
www.christinawright.squarespace.com
0204

Vanessa Yanow, Canada
vanessayanow@gmail.com
www.vanessayanow.com
0351, 0425, 0472

Limor Yaron, Product Designer,
Israel
Design@limoryaron.com
www.limoryaron.com
0488

YESDESIGNGROUP, USA
chrystal@yesdesigngroup.com
www.yesdesigngroup.com
0195

Melanie Young, Pieces of You,
Australia
piecesofyou32@yahoo.com
www.piecesofyou.typepad.com
0278–0281

Your Secret Admiral, USA
julie@yoursecretadmiral.com
www.yoursecretadmiral.com
0027, 0040, 0044, 0046, 0051

Joanne Zdrojewski, USA
www.joanofz.etsy.com
0091

Sebastian Zehe, Germany
www.flickr.com/photos/
threeheadedmonkey
0546, 0608

Hongtao Zhou, USA
lifeisfurniture@gmail.com
0978, 0979

**Romy Sai Zunde, Insectus
Artefacts,** Australia
dr.insectus@gmail.com
www.insectus.etsy.com
0326, 0334, 0448, 0477, 0926

ABOUT THE AUTHOR

Garth Johnson is a studio artist, writer, and assistant professor at College of the Redwoods in Eureka, California. In addition to maintaining the website Exteme Craft (www.extremecraft.com), Garth has written for magazines, museum catalogs, and books worldwide, including *CRAFT* and *Readymade* magazines and the companion volume to Faythe Levine's *Handmade Nation* documentary. His first DVD, *ReVision: Recycled Crafts for Earth-Friendly Living,* was released by Eyekiss Films in April 2009. When he's not teaching or decorating porcelain plates with a paintball gun, Garth can be found on the road giving his lecture "The Extreme Craft Roadshow." He is currently developing a lecture about the history of creative reuse to complement this book.

ACKNOWLEDGMENTS

This book would not have been possible without the kind support of fellow craft writers/bloggers like Tsia Carson (Supernaturale.org), Dennis Stevens (RedefiningCraft.com), Betsy Greer (Craftivism.com), and Maria Elena Buszek (Extra/Ordinary: Craft and Contemporary Art). I am also forever indebted to these kind people for helping to spread the word about the book: Natalie Zee Drieu, Rachel Hobson, Becky Stern, Doug Gunzelmann, Cyndi Lavin, Adam Williams, Treehugger.com, Jeanee Ledoux, Amy Shaw, Kim Dorn, Shauna Lee Lange, Becky Striepe, Danielle Maveal, and Leah Kramer. I would also like to thank my students and colleagues at College of the Redwoods in Eureka, California, for their contributions and support.

As scary and unlikely as it might sound to him, I would like to thank Henry Owings of *Chunklet* magazine for being a great role model. Namita Wiggers of the Portland Museum of Contemporary Craft generously took time out of her busy schedule to edit my introduction and help me organize my thoughts. My thanks also go out to Quarry/Rockport's amazing team: Cora Hawks, Tiffany Hill, and their amazing book designer, Sandra Salamony. My editor, Mary Ann Hall, is responsible for planting the initial seeds for this book, and I thank her for being its tireless champion. Finally, I would like to thank my long-suffering wife, Claire, who helped me in more ways than I could possibly list here.